Marco Gasparini

THE MAFIA
HISTORY AND LEGEND

Flammarion

CONTENTS

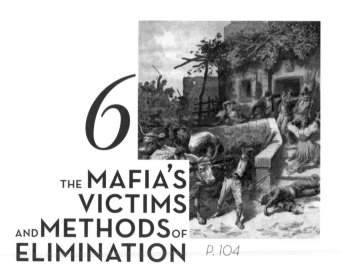

INTRODUCTION

"The Mafia," according to Judge Giovanni Falcone, "is not invincible. It was made by men and, like all things made by men, it had a beginning and it will have end." But the final word on the Mafia has not been written; not in Sicily where it was born, nor in other nations that are home to similar criminal organizations. These include the Japanese Yakuza, the Chinese Triads, the Russian Mafia, and those in the Balkans which, for historic, social, and economic reasons, have become a true "state within the state."

The Sicilian Mafia and its twin, the American Cosa Nostra, have histories that have always been intertwined with a mythology that set them apart from other criminal groups. In little more than one hundred and fifty years the Sicilian-American Mafia has given rise to a true international empire of crime that operated within different structures but always had a common goal. This was, simply, to become rich, thanks to an extraordinary ability to interact as equals with politicians and men in charge of official institutions, and to use all available financial means in order to consolidate power.

There are always historians ready to maintain that the Cosa Nostra was involved in the Allied landings in Sicily in 1943. Other scholars believe that the Sicilian Mafia was implicated in the slaughter at Portella della Ginestra, carried out four years later by Salvatore Giuliano and his gang. That massacre of peasants was supposedly part of a wider anti-communist strategy, carried out by the secret services of the West to guarantee

Italy's political stability when it was about to join NATO in opposition to the Soviet bloc.

Somewhere along the (sometimes subtle) line that separates the history of the Cosa Nostra from its mythology are those who attest that a plot by politicians and the Mafia was behind the assassination of President John F. Kennedy in 1963. The ties between the Sicilian Mafia and corrupt government officials would resurface in 2009, following revelations of presumed talks between the Italian state and the Corleone gangs. These talks were meant to put a halt to the new period of violence that began after the murders of Giovanni Falcone and Paolo Borsellino in 1992,

The crime association. Lucky Luciano (third from the left), financial brains of the Cosa Nostra, and Meyer Lansky (fourth from the left) who transformed the Mafia into a multinational crime syndicate, pose next to other bosses during Prohibition: Paul Ricca (left), member of "The Outfit" (the Chicago Mafia); Salvatore Agoglia (second from the left); John Senna (fifth from the left) and Harry Brown (right).

and the attacks on monuments in Rome and Florence in 1993.

Among the many theories and conjectures that surround the history of the Cosa Nostra there are, nevertheless, certain facts that clearly demonstrate its power and the danger it presents. Godfathers and Mafia bosses, together with the "white collars" who watch out for their financial interests, today manage a business turnover that is undoubtedly greater than that of the other criminal organizations.

Meanwhile the Neapolitan Camorra is still active, as is the Calabrian 'Ndrangheta that advances threateningly towards the rest of Europe: it was responsible for the massacre in Duisburg,

Germany, in 2007, and it continues to launder enormous amounts of illegal capital through legitimate financial circuits. It will, as Falcone said, be possible to write the last word on the Mafia, but only if there is a marked change in the mentality which still appeals to the fantasies of the new generations of Mafiosi. The first danger to avoid is to think that these criminal organizations are somehow glamorous and attractive, let alone mere museum pieces which are restricted by their geographical boundaries. This book endeavors to show the reader the real face of the Mafia: the first step towards attempting to change any human phenomenon is an accurate knowledge of it.

THE **ORIGINS** OF THE **MAFIA**

The historical, political, and economic roots of the Mafia. The unwritten rules, rituals, and moral codes of the Mafia, and its ties with the poorest regions of southern Italy. Other Italian criminal groups: the Camorra in Naples, the 'Ndrangheta in Calabria, and the Sacra Corona Unita ("United Sacred Crown") in Puglia.

A Code of Honor from the Past

At eighteen minutes past eleven on the morning of April 11, 2006, the feast day of St. Stanislaus, in a cottage clinging to a hillside in the town of Corleone, in the Montagna Cavalli district of Palermo, the police arrested Bernardo Provenzano after forty-three years of evasion. The officers were at the head of a task force made up of twenty-eight men, some of whom had been assigned from Rome.[1]

Provenzano, the ultimate prize of the Mafia*, a boss of bosses* of the Cosa Nostra*, fell into a trap in the same region that saw the start of his criminal career. The network of protection and complicity that had assured his liberty for decades had finally been broken through a series of wiretaps. The police had tracked him down to the farmhouse by intercepting the coded messages exchanged by his accomplices. Their loyalty was beyond reproach; they brought food and clothing to Provenzano's mountain hideaway, and then carried away the death sentences he issued. Among the items found by police in the three rooms that made up the cottage were two typewriters, one an electronic model, Brother AX-410, and the other a traditional Olivetti with ribbon.[2] Scattered about were the tiny sheets of paper used by the Mafia for secret communication and known as *pizzini*, covered in a code known only to a select few. The windows were concealed by lengths of cloth, and the door had a peephole that allowed the inhabitants to look out without being seen.

The house itself belonged to a forty-two-year-old shepherd who also ended up in handcuffs. Were it not for the vacation homes that had begun to dot the surrounding hillsides, the house might resemble an outpost on a large feudal estate. It was like so many of the farmhouses scattered in the hinterlands of Palermo, Trapani, and Agrigento, where the

There are many theories about the origins of the Mafia, many of which emphasize a particular ideology. One such theory, which sees the roots of the Mafia originating in the thirteenth century with the Sicilian Vespers of 1282, makes a clear connection between the Mafia and Sicilian nationalism. The rebellion, which was sparked off following the alleged attack of a French soldier on a young noblewoman, set off a popular revolt against Sicily's Angevin rulers that lasted for several days and resulted in many casualties. Painting by Domenico Morelli (1826–1901).

Mafia found fertile ground for its development and from which it was able to extend its tentacles first to other parts of Sicily, and then on to the United States during the waves of migration that occurred at the turn of the twentieth century.

Any history of the Italian Mafia must analyze above all a particular mentality, one that has it roots in, and in many ways still belongs to, a bygone era. In an attempt to understand relationships and the powerful connections that govern them, such a history must describe a specific way of life, one governed by a series of unwritten laws parallel to and stronger than the official rules. These relationships and codes create, in effect, a parallel state, one that exists alongside the official state.[3] This parallel state is able to infiltrate official institutions in order to corrupt and then exploit them, consolidating positions of power and prestige to extract maximum profit,[4] with no regard to human cost.

Problematic Origins

The very concept of the Mafia is multifaceted and refers, more than anything else, to a cultural framework deeply informed by ancestral attitudes and behaviors, as well as the result of a long and complex series of social transformations. Equally complex are the theories surroundings its origins, and the etymology of its name, which continue to be debated by scholars today (see "Mafia: The Name and Dialect", p. 28). Among the many theories devoted to the subject, some trace the origins of the Mafia to the late 1200s, when Sicily was ruled by the French Angevins and Palermo became a site of unrest during the popular uprising

known as the Sicilian Vespers.[5] The revolt began on the evening of March 31, 1282, in the courtyard of the Church of the Holy Spirit. According to a version by Bartolomeo Neocastro da Messina, who took part in the rebellion, a young French soldier named Drouet molested a Sicilian noblewoman in the company of her husband, on the pretext of searching for weapons that she might have been hiding under her wide skirts.[6] Her husband attacked the Frenchman, killing him, and when his compatriots tried to avenge his death, the local men from the village retaliated, sparking off a violent reaction against French rule that left, according to some historical accounts, two thousand Frenchmen dead by the following morning.

This attempt to link the Mafia's beginnings to episodes of Sicilian independence emerges in other theories and is perhaps the result of an unconscious aim of ennobling its origins by linking it to an attractive ideology. The roots of the Mafia have also been linked to secret societies, specifically the secret organization known as the Vendicosi, which first appeared in the thirteenth century and whose members were known to use any means necessary to fight the abuse of power. Later, in the seventeenth century, the Mafia was linked to an insurrectionist organization known as the Secret Confraternity of the Blessed Pauls,[7] whose followers held their covert meetings in underground crypts in Palermo.

This indirect association between various secret brotherhoods, religious sects, and the Mafia would later be officially documented. In 1838, for example, Pietro Calà Ulloa, the king of Naples's prosecutor, sent a document to the minister of justice of Ferdinand II, king of the Two Sicilies.

The Mafia is something distinct from common banditry, which in Italy has ancient roots and its own legends. In this image, Ludovico Ariosto (1474-1533), the author of the epic chivalric poem Orlando Furioso, is surrounded by bandits who honor him. Engraving from around 1833.

ARIOST.

Carlsruhe im Kunst-Verlag, Creuzbauer.

In his report on the political and economic condition of Sicily, he refers, among other things, to a "type of sect" found in various parts of the territory, which operates under the authority of a *capo*, or leader. These "unions—or brotherhoods" the document continues, have no "political affiliation or purpose" and make their appearance when the situation is one of "general corruption"[8] and people have no faith in official institutions or upholders of the law. These groups then offer their influence and help to the victims of crimes, allowing them, for example, the chance to recover their possessions or other forms of retribution.

The Mafia Establishes its Territories

"The Mafia is a state of mind that goes back to the Middle Ages." "A mafioso is someone" who operates "independently of the actions of the authorities and the law,"[9] and who exercises absolute power in his territory in order to resolve the "questions of love" and "interests"[10] that create quarrels and discord among local communities. These definitions date from 1876, and consolidate ideas about and modes of behavior by the Mafia dating back over centuries. They can be found in a two-volume investigation carried out by two young scholars from Tuscany, Leopoldo Franchetti and Sidney Sonnino. They were later conservative members of the Chamber of Deputies of the Kingdom of Italy, which Sicily joined after the plebiscite of October 21, 1860, immediately after the defeat of the Bourbons by Garibaldi, and Sidney Sonnino would twice serve as prime minister of Italy in the early 1900s. In the late nineteenth century Franchetti and Sonnino

traveled under escort throughout Sicily, even in those areas of the countryside where the Mafia had become deeply rooted and where bandits, who were protected and controlled by gangs, committed robberies, livestock theft, kidnappings and murder.

The resulting report on their travels cast disturbing light on the political and administrative conditions in Sicily. These were well known to the central government in Rome, which was

Facing page: A gabellotto—or estate leaseholder—from the area of Sciacca, near Agrigento. These new figures arrived on the scene in the nineteenth century with the breakdown of the feudal system, and were able to drive out the great landowners, which in turn gave rise to the Mafia in the countryside of western Sicily. Nineteenth-century engraving.

Top and bottom right: Private guards and soldiers on horseback obeyed the orders of the gabellotti and made up part of the chain of command of the rural Mafia.

already deeply worried by the spread of violence in the south, which was practically out of control. But Franchetti and Sonnino were received in an atmosphere of reassuring hospitality, and had no need for weapons. There was no need to defend themselves, and, in any event, weapons could not help them understand that the Mafia drew its sustenance from those very hamlets, set in a barren, isolated countryside where criminal gangs were master and peasants continued to live in miserable conditions under constant threat of blackmail and intimidation. While wealthy landowners lived far away in luxurious palaces surrounded by palm trees or citrus orchards, bands of armed men protected their land. Between them, was an unwritten but ironclad pact, just as binding as any official law. And this pact commanded a respect even greater than gunfire. In exchange for protecting his land and controlling the workers, the landowner offered these armed guards, often convicted criminals, not only an opportunity to profit from the land, but also, and most importantly, the freedom to act with impunity because of the landowner's connections with the authorities.

The system of great landed estates in Sicily goes back to ancient times. Beginning with the Phoenicians, and then continuing with the Greeks, Carthaginians, and finally the Romans,[11] untilled raw land was granted by the state to local notables in exchange for a portion of the produce grown on it (known as a *decima*, meaning a tithe, or tenth part), and thanks, of course, to slave labor. But it was around the year 1100, under the Normans, that a feudal system was first established and would continue under the later rules of the Swabians and Bourbons. Under this system, a baron would take possession of new lands through direct investiture by the sovereign, or by acquiring them directly from the state, which was always willing to grant them for an advantageous price. Many of the barons exercised both penal and civil jurisdiction over their vassals, especially due to rights granted during the reigns of Philip III (1578–1621) and Philip IV of Spain (1605–1665). Even the governors of Sicily had to give way to the barons' power, as illustrated by the instructions given to the viceroys of Sicily in the seventeenth century by the Count-Duke of Olivares (1587–1645) when he warned that "with the barons you are everything; without them you are nothing."[12] This complete dominance of landed estates would continue, on paper, until the nineteenth century, but endured unofficially for quite some time beyond that.

Control of the Land

In 1812 a new constitution was approved in Sicily, along the lines of the constitutional monarchy in Great Britain, and in which the barons renounced their feudal rights. Those rights, although now abolished by law, nevertheless became, almost intact, part of the rules that would govern land use. In the interior regions of Sicily, this ancient feudal system would resist even the popular uprisings of 1820 and 1848. The alliance between barons and bands of private guards—by now actual armed groups used to maintain control on the estates—became part and parcel of a new system that was legal only at face value. And although the bonds of subjugation that had previously tied peasants to landowners were now officially broken, they now

The government sides with the landowners: the cabinet of General Roberto Morra di Lavriano, who was given full powers by the king of Italy in order to put down, with violence, the revolt known as the Fasci Siciliani, organized by the Sicilian workers' movement from 1891 to 1894. Drawing by D. Paolucci.

took the form of a lease contract mediated by a new figure known as a *gabellotto**. He undertook to manage the land, either to cultivate it directly or to allow third parties to use it, to produce a profit that would pay the landlord his fee (known as the *gabella*, an old word for a tax) as well as the costs of maintaining the men under his command. These included supervisors as well as armed guards on horseback, who oversaw the workers. At the base of the pyramid were the peasants, treated cruelly by the *gabellotti* and their thugs, exploited and forced to work under conditions that were little different from those of the past, and at wages so low that they often had to borrow money at extortionate rates. In addition to their duties, the *gabellotti* managed the swift transformation from simple renters into landowning proprietors, thanks to the capital they accumulated running the estates. The barons, no longer in control, were driven away from these lands, which had become for them sources of debt and personal misfortune. The *gabellotti* were thus able to acquire vast estates at rock-bottom prices,

Like many other cities, Castelvetrano, in the province of Trapani, joined the popular protest movement and was the scene of violent riots in 1893. Sicily was in a state of siege. An end to the disorder came only with military intervention. Drawing by D. Paolucci.

The streets of Castelvetrano (1893).

Left: A rock salt mine in Calabria. The carusi—boy laborers—of the sulfur mines in Sicily worked in similar conditions.

Facing page: A scene from the trial of Giuseppe De Felice Giuffrida, the Socialist deputy who received a heavy sentence for being among those who inspired the Fasci Siciliani. The amnesty that was granted to all the accused reduced his prison sentence considerably.

sometimes by threats of violence or kidnapping, often carried out by gangs that, just a short time earlier, had been working for the very people now being threatened.[13]

The Evolution of the Mafia as a Social Phenomenon

But the pyramidal structure of the rural gangs which so dominated the countryside, and which is often seen to provide the model for the Mafia's organization, coincides only in part with the image of the Mafia that we have today. Today's Mafia is less pyramid than octopus, capable of penetrating both the landscape and society by means of a complex network of relationships that moves from below (the underworld) to the uppermost reaches of official institutions above,[14] according to the ruthless logic of profit-making. Furthermore, the dismantling of the feudal estates and the barons' need to defend their properties, even if it meant using the services of "unskilled workers" provided

by the criminal gangs, does not completely explain why the Mafia was from the very beginning rooted in the western part of Sicily and not, for example, in eastern Sicily or in other areas of Europe where the feudal system of the ancien régime was collapsing under the weight of similar social transformations.[15] An understanding of the origins of the Mafia in the most modern sense of the term must therefore take into account many other factors.[16] It should be sought not only in the poverty and isolation of the countryside but also in those areas close to the city of Palermo where, from the early eighteenth century, the industrial cultivation and trade in citrus fruit began to flourish. Accordingly, it was with the "Mafia of the Gardens" (see p. 29) in the Conca d'Oro outside Palermo that the structure of the so-called honorable society became more sophisticated and ready to jump to the next level to become an outright criminal enterprise.[17]

At this time, therefore, a member of the Mafia would have taken on a more complex role.

In the guise of either a *gabellotto*, a *campiere** (armed guard), a brigand, or even the man who looks after the grounds of an estate, he might be a source of trouble, but he might also be the intermediary to whom people would turn in order to solve problems that can arise when duly constituted authority has neither the ability nor the desire to uphold the law. In this situation, the most basic rights can be interpreted as privileges, and such privileges are granted thanks only to the intercession of the Mafia, with its own notions of benevolence and mercy. A mafioso was someone who would intervene to settle a dispute, or avenge an insult to one's wife. He would take from the rich barons and give to the poor peasants. Or he would rid the countryside of *scassapagghiari* (literally those who "ruin the straw," i.e., petty thieves). The reason for the policing of petty thieves, however, was not entirely altruistic: such young men, while ransacking farms in search of food and drink, drew the attention of the authorities, which interfered with the activities of illegal traffickers. The picture that emerges of the role of the Mafia in such communities is therefore quite diverse. By the mid-nineteenth century there was already a "white-gloved high Mafia*"[18] that operated at the upper reaches of the criminal hierarchy and consisted of landowners, *gabellotti*, notable professional people, and corrupt government functionaries. Associated with them was a "low Mafia" composed of followers or soldiers who had no scruples and were skillfully manipulated from above as effective tools of "local government."[19]

Elusive justice. The conviction of the Sicilian deputy Raffaele Palizzolo for instigating the murder of Emanuele Notarbartolo was overturned due to insufficient evidence.

The Siege and Conquest of the Unified Italian State

Immediately following the unification of Italy, the Mafia began to conquer ever larger areas of land. Franchetti and Sonnino described the social and political climate in southern Italy as one in which the prefects, carabinieri, and police forces sent by the central government in Rome to impose and maintain the new order struck "the same pose as would a statue of justice set in the middle of a band of criminals." They described these "new invaders" as living among "the population, isolated as if in a desert, seeing and hearing but without understanding." They accused them of being "ignorant of the language, the places, and the people" and of that "second language spoken with gestures and a turning away of the eyes" by which the Mafia warns its members of approaching danger.[20]

Helping to spread the Sicilian people's discontent with the authorities, and to swell the ranks of the Mafia, was the central government in Rome itself, which at the end of the nineteenth century used violent force to crush the latest in a series of popular revolts in Sicily against oppression of the lower classes. The crackdown was caused by a revolt inspired by the workers' movement known as the Fasci Siciliani in 1894 and ended with the sentencing of several of the movement's political representatives, along with some from the labor unions, among them the Socialist deputy Giuseppe De Felice Giuffrida (1859–1920).[21] Giuffrida suffered under the repression of Premier Francesco Crispi's government and was sentenced by a military tribunal in Palermo to eighteen years in prison. However, having maintained his independence from his party's official cadres, Giuffrida was pardoned and spent only two years in jail. (He would go on to be elected president of the province and mayor of the city of Catania at the head of its first leftist administration.) The link between the Mafia and legitimate politicians would therefore take its cue from the unstated need of central government to oppose the advance of socialism and communism in southern Italy.

But this was only one of several causes for impatience on the part of the Sicilian people. Beyond the problem of agrarian reform, there was a need to address the inhuman working conditions in Sicily's sulfur mines,[22] where young boys, known as *carusi*, and generally between eight and eleven years old, were forced to work with pickaxes in order to excavate the mineral from the mine tunnels.[23] Working almost naked in the hellish underground heat, and loading almost sixty-five pounds on their backs at a time, these *carusi* were links in a chain of exploitation that in the early twentieth century came to involve even the Mafia, as a result of the steep rise in the demand for minerals needed during World War I. Such inhuman conditions were found not only in Sicily but also in the rock salt mines of Calabria, where children of all ages were employed.

The link between the Mafia and the political class began to infect other nerve centers vital for control of the economy. The bosses soon turned to the finance of public works projects, at the time managed by the Bank of Sicily. It was no coincidence that the bank featured in a famous trial of 1899 involving several members of the Mafia following the murder of Marquis Emanuele

Picciotti is a term that refers both to low-level mafiosi and to Sicilians who fought with Garibaldi. The Mafia recruited its soldiers both from Garibaldi's men and from those who were dodging the draft to avoid serving in the army of the new Kingdom of Italy.

Notarbartolo,[24] the bank's governor. Committed to improving the bank's fortunes, Notarbartolo had embarked on an intense program of reorganization and recovery based on standards of transparency and efficiency. This immediately put him in conflict with local notables whose interests were not quite so clean. On February 1, 1893, Notarbartolo was stabbed twenty-seven times while on a train traveling between Termini Imerese and Trabia. Two men connected to the Sicilian gangs were charged with the murder, and in 1899 the Chamber of Deputies authorized the prosecution of one of its own members, Raffaele Palizzolo, as the instigator of the crime. Palizzolo was convicted in 1901 but acquitted four years later by the Court of Assizes in Florence due to insufficient evidence.

Bandits and Other Criminal Organizations in Southern Italy

The Mafia is not simply a criminal group, but a phenomenon deeply embedded within the culture, territory, and social fabric of Sicily. For this reason it must be distinguished from the banditry[25] that was of concern throughout Italy especially in the nineteenth century. This banditry often had revolutionary objectives and sometimes operated in disguise, as, for example, with the monk's habit worn by Michele Pezza, known as Frà Diavolo (1760–1806). Pezza was a pro-Bourbon royalist brigand and renegade monk who was put to death in Naples by the French for inciting rebellion. The Mafia behaves differently from such revolutionary bandits, however, and the difference extends to other organizations that appear outwardly similar to the Sicilian gangs, such as the 'Ndrangheta* in

Le Petit Journal
ADMINISTRATION — 5 CENT. SUPPLÉMENT ILLUSTRÉ 5 CENT. ABONNEMENTS
22me Année — DIMANCHE 26 MARS 1911 — Numéro 1.062

LE PROCÈS DE LA CAMORRA
Les accusés enfermés dans la « gabbione »

Calabria, the Sacra Corona Unita* in Puglia, and the Camorra* in Naples. This last group shares the greatest number of similarities with the Mafia, both in structure and in the scale of the hierarchical system that links its members in an unbreakable bond of blood and mutual loyalty. It was no coincidence that the Camorra established itself in Campania during the same period[26] as the Mafia, helped perhaps by the intermingling of Sicilians and Neapolitans due to the continuous exchange of government personnel during the period of the Kingdom of the Two Sicilies in the first half of the nineteenth century.[27]

The Mafia and the Camorra: A Shared Code of Honor

There are many similarities between the Mafia and the Camorra in their use of violence and blackmail as a means of intimidation and to extract profit, but each has origins in a specific society, with its own moral codes. In Naples, for example, there was a long tradition of inflicting scars as punishment for transgressive behavior. A woman accused of infidelity, for example, would have her face cut with a knife (a punishment known as a *sfregio d'amore,* or love scar), and the same could happen to those accused of insubordination (in this case the punishment was known as *sfregio a comando,* or disloyalty scar), such as being rude to a boss or refusing to carry out an order. Between 1830 and 1840, the inflicting of scars for punishment and intimidation became so common in Naples that the authorities were forced to intervene in an attempt to repress the barbaric custom.[28] Fines for inflicting such punishments were increased, along with random searches for weapons, although members of the Camorra managed to avoid detection by substituting small coins with razor-sharp edges for knives.

This climate of heavy social subjugation led to more serious crimes, and yet, when the interests of the Camorra were at stake, it was very difficult to reach a guilty verdict. One trial in particular stands out as an example[29]: On June 6, 1906, the body of Gennaro Cuocolo was found in the town of Torre del Greco, near Naples, repeatedly beaten and stabbed. A few hours later the body of his wife, Maria Cutinelli, was found stabbed in an apartment in Naples. They had been working for the Camorra, assisting in local robberies by providing tips about elegant homes, along with molds of door locks for making duplicate keys. The police were the first to investigate the double homicide of a this pair of petty criminals but the case was soon revealed to be more complicated than expected, and, after a series of arrests the investigators found themselves at a dead end. At this point the investigation was handed over to the local carabinieri, who accused the previous investigation of inefficiency and corruption. This time, thanks to the assistance of an informer named Gennaro Abbatemaggio, the carabinieri were able to reconstruct the crime. The Cuocolos were killed on orders from the Camorra because they were thought to be double agents providing information to the authorities. On October 22, 1907, the deputy prosecutor general in Naples put some forty-seven defendants on trial. The case, tried in the city of Viterbo near Rome for reasons of security, ended with mass convictions, with the defendants sentenced to a total of 354 years in prison. Fifteen years after that dramatic moment, however, Abbatemaggio, one of the first of the Camorra *pentiti,* recanted all his accusations, which had probably been extracted under duress. Despite this, the case was never reopened.

The Camorra punished transgressors in a very visible way, scarring the faces of women accused of being unfaithful, or of anyone who disobeyed its orders.

Left: Convictions
and acquittals.
The sentence
handed down in 1912
by a court in Viterbo
against the accused
in the Cuocolo case
was reversed
after Gennaro
Abbatemaggio
recanted his
statement.

Facing page: The
body of Maria
Cutinelli, stabbed
in her apartment
by the Camorra.

THE NAME AND DIALECT

The word *maffia* appears in a document for the first time in 1658, a slang term for a woman who practiced magic.[1] But it was not to appear in a dictionary of the Sicilian dialect until 1868, when it was defined as meaning misery, and was believed to have been imported from Tuscany by the natives of Piedmont who came to Sicily following in Garibaldi's wake. Other interpretations trace the origins of the word back to the period of Muslim rule in Sicily during the ninth to eleventh centuries, linking it to the term *marfud*, from which the Sicilian *marpiuni* (swindler, crafty person) or *marpiusu-mafiusu*[2] might be descended. Another possibility is the Arab word *mahias*, whose meaning is linked to ideas of beauty, perfection, generosity, and a desire for freedom from oppression. Yet another interpretation defines *mahias* as a stone quarry, a reference to the places where rebel bands organized by the local Mafia chiefs to help Garibaldi's army would gather and take refuge.

All of these interpretations connect with the self-aggrandizing image projected by the gangs, and can be seen to connect, even tangentially, with ideas of honor and of rebellion. (Locally these criminal gangs are known as *cosche**, a Sicilian term that refers to the crown of leaves on an artichoke and which symbolizes the group's unity.) If the origins of the name are difficult to pin down, the Mafia has a slang[3] that is almost incomprehensible to an outsider. For example, *pezzu di 90* indicates a political faction, *tappu d'aciu* (manhole) refers to a carabiniere, *zaffa* (no specific meaning) to the police, and *astutato* (extinguished) to a dead person killed by a shotgun, to name but a few.

1. Leonardo Sciascia, "La storia della mafia," in *Storia illustrata* (Milan: Mondadori, April 1972), 34.
2. Salvatore Lupo, *History of the Mafia* (New York: Columbia University Press, 2009), 49.
3. Michele Pantaleone, The Mafia and Politics (New York: Coward-McCann, 1966), 22 ff.

THE MAFIA OF THE GARDENS

In the mid-1800s the valley that surrounds Palermo, known as the Conca d'Oro, appeared to travelers as a kind of Garden of Eden, in stark contrast with the barren and desolate reality of the nearby large landed estates. Expanses of vineyards, gardens, and orchards supported a flourishing agriculture dedicated above all to the cultivation of citrus. Cargo ships sailed from Palermo for London and New York, loaded with crates of produce for the international market. By the end of the previous century, the British Royal Navy was already supplying its ships with enormous quantities of lemons in order to prevent scurvy, a disease caused by malnutrition and a lack of vitamin C. In the year 1840, an essential oil derived from another citrus fruit, the bergamot, was first used in England as a flavor in the famous Earl Grey tea.[1] These factors contributed to making Palermo's Conca d'Oro one of the most prosperous agricultural regions of Europe at the time, superior in yield even to the rich orchards that surrounded Paris during that same period. By the time the kingdom of Italy was established in 1861, more than 10 percent of a population of some 200,000 people in Palermo[2] made their living from the land. The properties were mostly owned and managed by small entrepreneurs, unlike the large landed estates. But the orchards, besides being extraordinarily productive due to the enormous initial investments made in them, also had a weakness: in order to develop and prosper they needed water, especially during the critical parts of the season. The caretakers of the wells, known as *fontanieri*,[3] after the word for fountain, along with those in charge of the gardens, known as *giardinieri*, besides being smugglers, thus became critical components of the Mafia groups that concerned themselves with citrus. The owners who resisted the rackets, which consisted of stealing crops as well as rake-offs on the sale of merchandise, had no way out: they could give in to blackmail or else see their crops dry up. They were helpless against threats to halt the irrigation and helpless against the guns that backed up the threats. The control of a network that was already at the center of bloody battles between gangs fighting over territory was entrusted to a group of unscrupulous businessmen and go-betweens who were linked together in a way which went further than the usual relationships between aristocrats and *gabellotti* that were typical of the large estates. Their impunity was guaranteed by a state that was weak, if not completely absent. The inhabitants of the villages were transformed into voter-subjects ruled and manipulated by the bosses and local notables who ended up in almost total[4] control of politics and institutions.

1. Vincenzo Ceruso, *Le sagrestie di Cosa Nostra* (Rome: Newton Compton editori, 2007), 29.
2 John Dickie, Cosa Nostra: A History of the Sicilian Mafia (New York: St. Martin's Press, 2004), 53 ff.
3 Lupo, 49.
4 Lupo, 118

THE MAFIA IN THE UNITED STATES

The emigration of organized crime from Italy to the United States and the birth of the Black Hand in New York. The link between Old World and New. The Mafia in New Orleans: the assassination of Chief of Police David C. Hennessy. Al Capone and Prohibition. Frank Costello and his slot machines. Vito Genovese, Carlo Gambino, and other Italian gangsters made in America.

The Arrival of Sicilian Immigrants and the Birth of the Black Hand in New York

Between 1876 and 1925, some 1.5 million Sicilian immigrants—almost two-thirds of those who left the island in search of a better life—made the journey to the United States. Between 1901 and 1914, when the wave of immigration reached its peak, eight hundred thousand Sicilians arrived in the United States,[1] driven by a deep economic depression and the government's harsh repression of the island's labor movement.[2]

Crammed almost beyond endurance on steamships leaving Europe, with suitcases, baskets, and cardboard trunks tied with string, this great sea of travelers came ashore on Ellis Island, the small island in Upper New York that, up until 1954, served as a reception center and hospital for those arriving in the United States. Starting in 1892, more than 12 million aspiring American citizens would pass through Ellis Island. Its records document the ethnic composition of these waves of immigration from the Mediterranean, as well as the criminal element that came with it. Concealed within the crowds of honest laborers were convicted criminals and fugitives on the run from the authorities in Sicily. That is not to say that Sicily was the sole origin of criminal immigrants: all ethnicities and nationalities had their criminal contingent who, as they arrived in the United States, would fight

Immigrants from southern Italy on their way to Canada pass through the train station in Milan. (Image taken from the Domenica del Corriere.*)*

Arriving at Ellis Island in New York. Hidden among the crowds of honest immigrants from Sicily were criminals sought by the Italian police.

Above left:
Immigrant families
carried all their
belongings in sacks
and suitcases tied
with string.

Right: Mulberry
Street, the heart
of New York's Little
Italy, in a photo
from around 1900.

for positions in the upper reaches of organized crime, creating networks and connections with local authorities in order to exploit the profits generated by prostitution, gambling, illegal lotteries, counterfeit currency, and smuggling.

Along with this wave of immigration to New York at the end of the nineteenth century, came a new threat. In the neighborhood between Mulberry and Elizabeth Streets known as Little Italy, a former slum improved by the Italian immigrants who had settled there, the merchants and small businessmen began to receive blackmail letters from a group calling itself La Mano Nera, or the Black Hand*. The group consisted mainly of recent immigrants from Sicily who specialized in extortion. The Black Hand took its name from the Mano Negra, a Spanish anarchist group of the eighteenth and nineteenth centuries. The Sicilian group sent letters demanding huge sums of money in exchange for protection from arson or bomb attacks, kidnappings or worse, all signed with a threatening drawing of a hand surrounded by skulls and daggers. This system of extortion was so far-reaching that it included among its victims the celebrated Italian tenor Enrico Caruso, from whom the racketeers

Caro Amico

Dopo d'avervi scritto parecchie volte
non vi siete benignato a farvi vivo
credete forse d'aver a che fare con
vigliacchi? In noi trovate uomini
di cuore e che abbiamo sangue
nelle vene, non miserabili come
voi, Aprite gli occhi questa è l'ultima
lettera che vi indirizziamo, e se non
porterete il Denaro sul posto dove
vi abbiamo detto raggerete il fio
col nostro consacrato pugnale
che vi spillerà una pinta di

Mercoledì prossimo

Alfred J. Young Collection, N.Y.C.

sangue dal vostro cuore.
Badate con chi avete a che fare
Noi non abbiamo paura della
vostra polizia. Lasciatela stare
in pace. Fateci guadagnar
da vivere.
Non fate orecchie da mercante
altrimenti vi faremo prelato
e dottore della chiesa.
Con noi non si fa cerimonie
di nessuna sorte e nemmeno
chiacchiere.
Vi diamo il tempo. Sino a
Mercoledì, al medesimo posto coi
prezzi segnali alla mezza notte
avete capito?
Se a questo ultimo puntamento
non siete puntuale potete

conturvi fra il numero dei morti
Sarete crivellato prima voi e poi
l'intera vostra famiglia.
Mentre noi con la nostra mano
potente non lasciamo traccie
alcuna, e dopo avervi scannati
come tante pecore adoperiamo
il nostro metodo della dinamite
cui farà sparire ogni piccola
brama di cuore

Uomo avvisato e mezzo
salvato, perciò se volete
comprarvi la morte porterete
il Denaro

Ci firmiamo

La Mano Nera

demanded—without success—the then-vast sum of five thousand dollars.[3]

The Black Hand had aspirations of spreading beyond New York, and expanded their empire to St. Louis, Kansas City, and Chicago. However, businessmen, tired of local government's powerlessness against the Black Hand, started an organization in retaliation: the La Mano Bianca, or the White Hand.[4] Meant to combat the Black Hand's extortion rackets, the White Hand* would lend money to those in financial difficulties who did not want to resort to usury. Such activities added impetus to the growing Nativist movement in the United States, which advocated for a majority presence of white native-born Protestants over the "new ethnic groups." Its supporters, active in politics, believed in a foreign conspiracy and called for drastic measures to curtail the flow of immigrants, resulting in actual exclusionist policies. The 1924 National Origins Act was one such measure, which set limits on the number of immigrants from eastern and southern Europe. The presence of the Black Hand soon began to diminish and eventually disappeared, but no thanks to such policies: it became absorbed by the extortion rackets run by the Sicilian-American Mafia.

Business Opportunities, Old and New

The link between the Old World and the New became stronger in the sphere of organized crime, thanks to the constant flow of young men with Mafia connections, often on the run from the Italian police, who were able to travel the United States to be of service to the countrymen already engaged in criminal activities there. These future workers in organized crime would cross in waves over that metaphorical bridge that still links the Sicilian Mafia to the families of the American Cosa Nostra, which had its beginnings in the United States in the late nineteenth century. In that period the "godfathers" began to assume a prominent role in the illegal trafficking that enabled the movement of great masses of people to the Americas. For large fees, these men would arrange for associates* of the gangs, for ordinary criminals, and for those fleeing military service or other fugitives, to board fishing boats in Mazara del Vallo, on Sicily's southern coast. The boats would head for Tunisia, often with livestock stolen from the countryside and intended for sale on the African market. In Tunisia, these illegal immigrants would meet steamers bound for New York by way of Marseille.[5] This chain of illegal activity often included "brokers" who specialized in finding work and lodgings for their fellow villagers once they arrived in America with the help of "sponsors" who were responsible for receiving them.[6] Added to this source of earnings were other equally profitable—and legitimate— commercial ventures: thanks to the network of family contacts that developed between New York and Sicily, many Sicilian families began to focus on the export of oranges and lemons to the United States, benefiting from the considerable advance payments offered by American importers in exchange for preferential treatment and the best quality merchandise.[7]

Extortion letter signed by the Black Hand. The practice of the pizzo, a sum of money demanded by the gangs from small businesses and already in use in southern Italy, was accompanied by threats and dynamite attacks in many U.S. cities.

The Mafia in New Orleans

Although geographically separated by thousands of miles, the Sicilian Mafia and the American Cosa Nostra shared similar customs and mechanisms that, at the end of the nineteenth century, seemed to have a natural affinity with the city of New Orleans. The economy of the jazz capital benefited massively from its bordellos and gambling establishments, which led to sometimes incendiary confrontations with the forces of law and order. On October 15, 1890, local Irish police chief and bounty hunter David C. Hennessy was mortally wounded by a pistol. His last whispered words, "Dagoes did it,"[8] (a pejorative term for immigrants from Italy), led to a sensational court case the following year, in which a not-guilty verdict led to the lynching of eleven Italians by an angry mob. Following the incident, the press used the word "Mafia" for the first time, introducing the term to the American public.

In truth, however, the incident marked the end of a long and bloody war between rival gangs fighting for control of the imported fruit market from Europe and South America, and which had been under investigation by Hennessy. At the time, the city's fruit and vegetable markets were firmly under the control of the Sicilian Provenzano gang, nicknamed the "Stoppaglieri" (related to Sicilian prison slang, *aviri stuppa* and *avere stuppa*, meaning to be able to keep a secret). An attempt to set up a racket in the same territory by a rival faction known as the Matranga gang (and nicknamed *giardinieri*, or gardeners) ended in bloodshed and the death of six people.

Hennessy had previously been celebrated in the newspapers for capturing Giuseppe Esposito, an infamous criminal from Calabria who was in hiding in the United States and still wanted in Italy in connection with eighteen murders and kidnapping with torture. But Hennessy was himself suspected of collusion with the Provenzano gang and so the investigations into his murder were directed at the members of the Matranga gang, conducted in an atmosphere of tense confrontation and intimidation of the city's Italian residents. The result was a witch hunt instigated by the unscrupulous mayor of New Orleans, Joseph A. Shakspeare and, in an attempt to appease the anger of many in the city, the investigators arrested eighteen members of the Matranga gang. The situation reached a bloody climax in mid-March 1891 when the grand jury acquitted seventeen of the eighteen murder suspects.[9] Almost immediately, the results of the trial were seen as suspect. It appeared that supporters of the Matranga had been able to collect seventy-five thousand dollars from various gangs to cover legal fees. The money was not only used to hire the best lawyers; there was the possibility it had been used to bribe some of the jurors.

The news was inflammatory. The anger of the local citizens spread in all directions, aimed even at new immigrants from Italy who, although they were both innocent and unaware of the situation, were greeted with hails of stones on their arrival. The local press incited the public to take justice into its own hands. On the morning of March 14, an angry crowd of some six thousand people marched to the prison where the acquitted were waiting to be freed. The prison superintendent, John Davis, unable to stop the immense crowd, tried to give the hunted men a means of escape through the women's area of the prison, but only a few succeeded in making

March 14, 1891: The assault on the prison in New Orleans. The killing of the Italians acquitted in the murder trial of Police Captain David C. Hennessy, and the subsequent waves of anti-Italian violence, were among the events that revealed the presence of the Mafia in the United States.

their way out. Of the eighteen men indicted for the murder, eleven could not escape a bloody lynching. The bodies of the victims, either dead or dying, were hung from trees on Trame Street, where they were shot by a platoon of thirty riflemen, selected from a watch committee. This horrific incident of mob rule was among the most savage in the entire history of the Italian-American Mafia. The events triggered a long-lived diplomatic crisis with the Italian government that would be resolved only after a decision by President Benjamin Harrison to offer compensation to the relatives of the victims.

A Criminal Bridge Between Past and Present

From the end of the nineteenth century, the incessant movement of immigrants between Italy and the United States, and sometimes back again, would consolidate the solid foundation and mutual kinships that bound the Sicilian-American Mafia. But the spread of the Mafia in America was more complicated than a simple transplant from the rural world of the Sicilian countryside to the urban United States. The American Mafia, known as the Cosa Nostra (literally "Our Thing") differed in its organizing and structural abilities, and it also differed from the Black Hand, which appeared in the United States at more or less the same time.

As with the early origins of the Mafia in Sicily, the early structure of the American Cosa Nostra also seems to have involved secret organizations. This covert activity was not motivated by any revolutionary impetus but instead as a necessary means for immigrant groups to make their way in a new world that appeared hostile and discriminatory.

The home grown American Mafia, founded and for the most part directed by Sicilians, found ways to adapt the customs and codes of behavior of rural Sicily to an environment that was highly industrialized. This was accomplished through the uninterrupted flow of contacts between groups in Sicily and the United States, and as a result of the mutual interests that they shared. The American Mafia also succeeded in establishing a truly capitalistic system[10] of a criminal type in a country that enjoyed the highest standard of living in the world. The Sicilian-American Mafia groups quickly tried to extend their tentacles to the most lucrative parts of the import-export trade, using a method of extortion much more refined than the brutal one practiced by the Black Hand. Other Mafia groups in the New World made their fortune in the lucrative trade of mail-order brides from Sicily, selected from photographs by criminals already in the United States.[11]

But the Sicilian-American Mafia was not the only organized criminal element in the United States, and it would engage in a prolonged struggle with Irish, German, and Jewish gangs for control of criminal activities. With this objective in mind, the bosses in the New World, following the model of their Sicilian cousins, would not hesitate to set in motion the gears of the political-electoral machine in the United States. This included the use of "repeaters" who would help rig an election by voting more than once[12] in order to secure victory for candidates favored by the gangs. They would also engage in activities that were only just the right side of legal, such as those connected with the Italian Lottery, an organization with ties to the Mafia that lent money at extortionate rates to the

Prohibition, which lasted from 1920 to 1933, opened the doors to a new and profitable criminal business for many groups of gangsters.

Left: Customs inspections and the confiscation of illegal goods did not stop the river of alcohol that flowed into the United States thanks to illegal imports by smugglers known as bootleggers.

Above right: One of the many secret distilleries that sprang up during Prohibition.

detriment of immigrant Italians. With the advent of Prohibition in 1920 they also tried to exploit, from the very beginning, the huge business that was bootlegged alcohol.

Prohibition and Al Capone

The crusade against the spread of immoral behavior and for the restoration of social order received a burst of energy on October 28, 1919, with passage by the United States Congress of the Volstead Act*. This legislation, which was to become law in all states on January 16, 1920, put into effect the rules on Prohibition contained in the Eighteenth Amendment to the United States Constitution. Some months earlier, that amendment had introduced a prohibition on the manufacture, transport, and sale of beverages containing more than 0.5 percent alcohol. The commissioner of the Internal Revenue Service (a bureau of the Department of the Treasury) was given extraordinary powers to guarantee the full application of the law in all states, including those in which the Anti-Saloon League did not have majority support.[13]

But contrary to its intent, the measure was like manna from heaven for organized crime. The demand for strong spirits, which was constantly on the rise, increased the price of a drink fourfold. As liquor became a genuine rarity, demand increased and a veritable river flowed secretly across the borders from Canada and Mexico, thanks to bootleggers* who smuggled the cases of precious

liquid to criminal groups who placed them on the American market at astronomical prices.[14] Illegal distilleries hidden within the country were also a huge source of income for crime bosses. In Austin, Texas, a distillery capable of producing up to 130 gallons of illegal liquor a day was discovered. Many Italian Americans, secure in the protection offered by the Unione Siciliana (an association established in New York for the purchase of life insurance but under the control of bosses such as Johnny Torrio, who used it for criminal and political purposes), could make what was known as bathtub gin for consumption at home and free from prosecution by the authorities. Among the tricks used to avoid attention from the police were pistols with barrels designed to incorporate a small flask. In New York, after ten years of Prohibition, some twenty thousand people[15] supposedly on the side of law and order were also on the payroll of organized crime bosses, willing to turn a blind eye to their activities. Many of them were policemen of Irish background, eager for a cut of the illegal profits.

In that same period, a gangster named Alphonse Gabriel Capone, better known as Al Capone, was making his way in Chicago.[16] According to the most accepted account, he was born on January 17, 1899, in Brooklyn, New York, where his family had arrived not long before from Italy, although some accounts maintain that he was born in Naples on January 6, 1895, in which case he might have arrived in the United States secretly together with his parents. Capone began his criminal career as a bouncer in a bar and brothel. Nicknamed "Scarface" because of a cut on the left side of his face, over the course of his life he was at the head of a gang with more than seven hundred members. He was involved in prostitution and gambling, and made millions, mainly due to bootlegged liquor. Protected by corrupt and obliging police, he managed to evade prosecution for years, claiming to be, as he loved to tell the press, "a businessman concerned only with satisfying the needs of the people."[17] Capone attracted the attention of an investigation by the U.S. government after the St. Valentine's Day Massacre of February 14, 1929, when six members of a rival gang headed by George "Bugs" Moran, were lined up against a wall in a Chicago garage and machine-gunned along with an innocent bystander.[18]

According to newspapers of the time, the victims, on the orders of Capone, were executed with .45-caliber Thompson submachine guns, sending out a clear signal that Capone didn't want any more interference with the growth of his business. Following the public outcry prompted by the massacre, President Herbert Hoover established a government task force assigned to arrest Capone.

Facing page:
Al Capone began his criminal career as a bouncer in a bar and ultimately made it to the top of organized crime, in part thanks to bootlegged alcohol.

Above right:
The St. Valentine's Day Massacre in a garage in Chicago on February 14, 1929.

The task force eventually succeeded in putting Capone behind bars, but not for the many crimes for which he was a suspect. Capone was arrested and found guilty of tax evasion, a crime that earned him a fine in the tens of thousands of dollars plus eleven years in prison, most of them spent in the federal penitentiary on Alcatraz Island. Capone died in January 1947, eight years after his release, in Florida, without ever returning to Chicago.

The Bosses of the New World

But Al Capone was not the only high-profile figure who traveled on that long road linking the Italian and American Mafias. There were many others, including Frank Costello, born in Calabria in 1891 and known as the prime minister of the underworld. Costello specialized in placing illegal slot machines in various family-run businesses in New York. It was an enterprise worth half a million dollars a day which, in 1934, prompted the newly elected mayor of New York, Fiorello H. LaGuardia, to start a campaign of moral reform directed against Costello's business. In front of a delighted press, LaGuardia literally took a sledgehammer to the slot machines and had them thrown in the river. The public gesture was unequivocal: LaGuardia's administration was nothing like his predecessor's, whose tolerance of the slot machines was indicative of far greater instances of corruption, in an era in which the local government (tightly controlled in that period by Tammany Hall, a political organization with ties to the Democratic Party) was synonymous with shady business deals, rigged elections, and the awarding of public contracts through patronage. Pressure from LaGuardia probably did not affect

Costello too greatly in the long run; he simply moved his operation to New Orleans, but still maintained connections in New York.

It was during the 1930s that the Commission of the Cosa Nostra*, the crime syndicate of the Italian-American Mafia, began to take shape, thanks to the initiative of "Lucky" Luciano.[19] The full extent of the organization would finally be revealed in 1985,

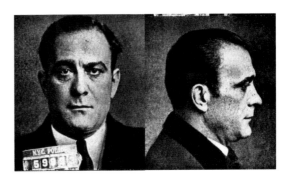

thanks to the efforts of future mayor Rudolph Giuliani (at the time a federal prosecutor in the Southern District of New York). The Commission aimed to guarantee peace between crime families in all parts of the country and also attempted to manage the illegal business interests in narcotics, gambling, and prostitution, without resorting to bloodshed. The Commission likewise was in charge of establishing territories and dividing up the various activities among the gangs, which were based on a formalized hierarchy of bosses, underbosses, lieutenants, and soldiers of the Cosa Nostra.

Vito Genovese, born in Naples in 1897, would aspire to reach the top of the Commission. But Frank Costello and Albert Anastasia had held that position since Genovese fled New York for Italy to escape a murder charge in 1937. On his return to New York in the 1950s, Genovese, who wanted,

Facing page: Frank Costello made his fortune in the gambling rackets. Together with Albert Anastasia he took command of the Cosa Nostra, the Italian-American crime syndicate.

Above right: Mafia wars. Vito Genovese in a police photo taken after his arrest in Italy in 1945. Extradited to the United States on a murder charge, for which he was acquitted, he then began a battle to topple Costello and Anastasia from their positions at the top of the Cosa Nostra.

among other things, to exploit the market for narcotics to the full, did everything he could to oust Costello and Anastasia from their positions of command. He arranged to have Anastasia shot, while at his barber's, on October 25, 1957. Costello was sufficiently shaken to concede his position without having to suffer the same fate.

In November of that year, a meeting was held in the town of Apalachin, New York. The purpose was to decide on a strategy for drug trafficking, after the passage of the Narcotics Control Act by Congress made it a federal crime. Genovese also planned to use the meeting to consolidate his position. But the presence of a state trooper ruined Genovese's plans for conquest: Edgar Croswell, spotting the large numbers of Mafia figures, called for reinforcements. Genovese was convicted in 1959 of drug trafficking and died in prison of a heart attack in 1969 in Springfield, Missouri.[20] As for Costello, he died of cancer in 1973.

His successor at age fifty-five was Carlo Gambino, born in Palermo on September 2, 1902. Modest and reserved in his demeanor, in the opinion of many he was the inspiration for the character of the godfather in Mario Puzo's famous novel of the same name. He would die of natural causes in Long Island at the age of seventy-four. In the early 1980s the Gambino name was involved in the criminal affairs of the "Pizza Connection*,"[21] a gigantic investigation into the heroin trade that would once more put the crime links between Italy and the United States in the media spotlight.

Other figures of greater or lesser importance in the Mafia hierarchy included Giuseppe Zangara, an immigrant from Calabria. The former marksman in the Italian army was sentenced to the electric chair in 1933 for an attempt on the life of President Franklin D. Roosevelt on February 15 of that year in Miami, Florida. Many believe that the actual target of the seven pistol shots was Anton Cermak, the mayor of Chicago and sworn enemy of the underworld bosses, including Frank Nitti, cousin of Al Capone. Cermak died from the serious wounds suffered while he walked at the president's side.

The last of the Sicilian-American godfathers to reach the top of the Cosa Nostra hierarchy was John Joseph "Johnny Boy" Gotti. Born in 1940, he ended up behind bars in 1992 when he received a life sentence for a triple homicide. After his death in prison from cancer, he was buried in St. John's Cemetery in New York in 2002. During the funeral, which cost some two hundred thousand dollars, twenty-two limousines followed his coffin as it traveled across Queens. Whether his death marks the end of the history of the Italian-American Mafia is anyone's guess.

Left: Anastasia arrived in the United States aged seventeen. Ambitious and ruthless, he was one of the main figures in the organized crime power structure that established itself with the various waves of immigration from Italy.

Facing page: Execution, Mafia style. Anastasia was killed in the Manhattan barbershop he frequented.

LUCKY LUCIANO
AND THE COSA NOSTRA
GET INVOLVED IN INTERNATIONAL POLITICS

The rise of Lucky Luciano in the Cosa Nostra and his control of the unions. The involvement of the Sicilian-American Mafia in the Allied landings in Sicily. Theories surrounding the Mafia and the assassination of President John F. Kennedy.

The deep economic crisis prompted by the collapse of the New York Stock Exchange on October 29, 1929, pushed the U.S. government to be more resolute in its fight against the corruption of the Prohibition years, and toward which the public was increasingly intolerant. The Eighteenth Amendment, which had prohibited the transport and consumption of alcoholic beverages, was repealed in December 1933. According to those in favor of repeal, the legalization of alcoholic beverages would guarantee thousands of new jobs[1] in a country that, at the height of the Depression, had 15 million unemployed (around 25 percent of the workforce). This prompted the Mafia bosses to focus on consolidating one of their other illegal activities as well as on developing new opportunities. The flow of mafiosi who came from Sicily on the "second wave" were attracted more by the opportunities of the United States[2] than repelled

by the Fascist repression on the island, and set in motion a new phase in the evolution of the Italian-American criminal underworld, under the influence of bosses such as Joe Bonanno and Salvatore Maranzano.

Bonanno and Maranzano were native-born Italians, men of the "old school" who spoke a strange form of broken English. They were known as "greasers" or "Moustache Petes" because of hair oil and long moustaches that they favored. Nonetheless, they were not stuck in the past: They laid the foundations for the modern Mafia in the creation of the Cosa Nostra Commission, formally initiated in the early 1930s by Lucky Luciano.

Born Salvatore Lucania in Sicily in 1897, Charles "Lucky" Luciano established the model of a Mafia based on a hierarchical structure similar to that of the Roman legions,[3] and open only to Italian Americans.

Lucky Luciano led the Cosa Nostra in a new direction, changing the standard model of the old Mafia and reducing the influence of tradition to make the structure and activities of the organization more international.

Left: Made in Italy. Joe Bonanno had a rather old-fashioned understanding of the Cosa Nostra as being an extension of the Sicilian families' tight network.

Facing page: Luciano was not afraid to be seen in public. It was a way of demonstrating his power and showing that the Mafia was untouchable. Here he takes a stroll in the company of his lawyer.

Lucky Luciano was responsible for creating the face of the modern crime syndicate,[4] known as the Commission, bringing together all the Mafia families, not just those from New York, but also those of Chicago (where the organization was called "the Outfit") and of Buffalo (where it was called "the Arm"). Among other things, he created the position of "consigliere*,"[5] a combination of diplomat and peacemaker, part of the structure of the Commission, as a way to avoid feuds* among the families. He internationalized the Sicilian-American Mafia by choosing as his right-hand man childhood friend Meyer Lansky (born Meyer Suchowljansky), a Jew of Byelorussian origin. Because of Luciano, the Mafia was able to interact on a higher level and in a more direct way with the "upper world" of legitimate institutions and businesses, but without sacrificing the Sicilian code of *omertà** or the organization's protection rackets.

As part of this modernization, it was also necessary to reduce the weight of the religious traditions that threatened to make the families of Sicilian origin too inward looking and less open to change. In *The Last Testament of Lucky Luciano*, the unauthorized biography by Martin Gosch and Richard Hammer,[6] Luciano recalls interior spaces that were practically covered with "crosses, religious images, and statues of the Virgin and of saints of whom I had never heard anyone speak." Concerning his rival Salvatore Maranzano, Luciano said that he "was the biggest fan of crosses in the world; he had them in his pockets and wherever he was there were crosses all over the place." Luciano wanted to minimize the hold such religious superstition had on his modern Mafia, but it was equally important that the Cosa Nostra did not sever all ties with its country of origin: its Italian identity was its trademark. It was also crucial that the rules first

The Mafia and
propaganda.
Luciano was willing
to give interviews
and seems to have
been behind the
unauthorized
biography The Last
Testament of Lucky
Luciano by Martin
Gosch and Richard
Hammer.

established in the Old World were still respected, particularly regarding *omertà* and loyalty to the organization. As Luciano often said, "The only way to leave the Mafia is in a coffin." At the same time, the American organization could not remain just a satellite of the one in Sicily.[7] It was because of this new setup that the independent mafiosi in America, while staying in very close contact with their native land, adapted themselves with great speed to the economic and social conditions of the New World.

The Rackets Muscle in on Legitimate Businesses

Parallel with the U.S. government's crackdown on crime, Luciano reinvested the stratospheric profits earned smuggling alcohol during Prohibition (12 million dollars in 1925 alone, Luciano claimed) in the new rackets of the twentieth century. The term "racket"—an uproar, or a noisy private party— gave birth to the noun "racketeer," which came to be used for a new category of criminal-manager involved in a whole host of illegal businesses such as usury, prostitution, drug trafficking, robbery, truck hijacking, and horse racing and lottery scams. It also included a more recent development in the labor market: the use of threats and extortion. This had been introduced by the Sicilian-American Mafia during the 1920s as part of its effort to control the Fulton Fish Market in New York[8] through the United Seafood Workers Union, whose members had the exclusive right to unload fishing boats from any part of the world. The means by which the bosses made money was simple: anyone who wanted to work in the port had to accept the wages set by the union. The increases in pay were minimal,

Meyer Lansky, Luciano's right-hand man, was the first financial genius of the Cosa Nostra.

which worked to the advantage of the businesses, who could count on a low-cost workforce. In exchange for money paid to the bosses, businesses were guaranteed freedom from strikes and other "incidents."

Luciano made the labor rackets even more effective through his close connections with the Jewish mobsters who kept the workers in Manhattan's textile industry in line through gangs of strikebreakers.[9] Luciano, who as a teenager had worked in the shipping department of a hat factory, became a powerful figure in the garment industry through his connection with the clothing workers union. He exploited the possibilities of the garment industry further by trafficking in heroin hidden in hat boxes.[10]

Meanwhile, other Sicilian-American bosses, in order to head off inquiries from the Inland Revenue, reinvested their earnings in businesses that were outwardly legitimate but that were used for Mafia concerns, such as the funeral parlor in Brooklyn that made coffins with false bottoms so that two bodies could be buried at the same time, allowing the corpses of those assassinated by the Cosa Nostra to disappear forever. But with the repeal of Prohibition and the crackdown on crime, Mafia organizations were forced to operate on a higher level.

On the Waterfront

The tentacles of the octopus would inevitably extend to the port of New York, where the Mafia was able to infiltrate the union known as the International Longshoremen's Association (ILA), whose membership included between thirty to

Period view of the port of New York, where the Mafia managed the import of illegal merchandise. Through its deep infiltration of labor unions, the Mafia controlled businesses and workers in a powerful mix of illegal activities.

forty thousand New York dockers, hired on a daily basis. The labor rackets operating on the docks, in particular on the piers in Brooklyn that were worked by Italians from the nearby neighborhood of Red Hook, had become a powerful bargaining tool between the union and City Hall and with import-export businesses.[11] The union promised to provide work for its members, who were divided into gangs and run according to a strict hierarchy. The businesses were willing to pay handsomely in order to secure protection from the threat of strikes, while the Mafia bosses, who had penetrated the upper reaches of the union, acted as mediators and profited by managing their own "traffic," for example drugs hidden in barrels of olive oil coming from Sicily.

The port area became critically important to the American government after the Japanese attack on Pearl Harbor on December 7, 1941. The involvement of the United States in World War II had a side effect of easing the pressure on organized crime that had, by this time, "reached alarming proportions compared to legitimate businesses."[12] The war also made the secure transport of troops and weapons to Europe by sea an important part of wartime strategy. The U.S. commanders, therefore, were concerned about the workers of German and Italian origin swarming the nation's docks. Many worried about the presence of Axis informers on American territory, and about the danger of sabotage to ships and supplies ready to leave for far-off theaters of operations.[13] Rumors abounded, for example, that fishing boats based in New York were stocked to secretly resupply German submarines stationed off the coast.

In this atmosphere of increasing anxiety, the mysterious sinking of the transatlantic liner *Normandie* in New York Harbor on February 9, 1942, prompted secret agents working for the U.S. Navy to seek a contact to the organized crime bosses who controlled the port.[14] They found that contact in Lucky Luciano, who was serving between thirty and fifty years in a maximum security prison as a result of his 1936 conviction for running a prostitution ring.

Dangerous Relationships

The actual purpose of and the circumstances surrounding Luciano's cooperation with the federal authorities have never been made clear. According to some theories, Luciano was of help in planning for the liberation of Sicily in 1943, thanks to his friendship with the Sicilian gangs.[15] But according to *The Last Testament of Lucky Luciano*, Luciano had been prohibited from "any kind of contact" with Sicily, which would have prevented him from having a role in the Allied landings in Sicily, codenamed Operation Husky*.[16] Nevertheless, some facts are not in doubt. Shortly after the start of his presumed cooperation with the authorities, Luciano was transferred from maximum security Dannemora Prison to the Great Meadow Correctional Facility in Comstock, New York (what has been described as being moved from "the Siberia of America" to "a country club"), and in 1946 he was deported from the United States. According to statements made to the 1951 U.S. Senate committee investigating organized crime led by Senator Estes Kefauver, Luciano was freed by the Americans shortly after

the war for the "valuable services rendered to the military authorities in regard to the plans for the invasion of his native Sicily." The information he provided, and above all his position inside the Cosa Nostra, served to "smooth the way for the American secret agents," making Sicily "a much easier objective" for the Allies.[17]

The Allied Landings in Sicily

The plans for the Allied invasion of Sicily had been decided in January in Casablanca by Franklin D. Roosevelt and Winston Churchill, after the defeat of the Axis forces in North Africa. The end of 1942 saw, among other things, an increase in espionage activity and reconnaissance on the part of submarines that managed to approach the coasts of Sicily undisturbed. After a period of intense bombardment, intended to soften up coastal defenses, the terrain would be prepared by raiders for the arrival of the troops.

Among the Americans under the command of General George S. Patton were several who spoke the Sicilian dialect.[18] They came from the area, had previously immigrated to the United States, and were now coordinating the assault troops, being familiar with the geography and local customs. They were also trying to contact gang members native to Sicily who had likewise immigrated to the United States but had been expelled.

Operation Husky began 10 July, 1943, at 2:45 a.m. It would be the dress rehearsal for Operation Overlord, which, almost one year later, on June 6, 1944, and much further north, would cover the beaches of Normandy in blood, open the road to Berlin for the Allies, and grip the Nazi-Fascist

A poster from 1935 shows the transatlantic liner Normandie, which mysteriously sank in New York Harbor. The incident prompted the authorities to contact the Mafia and ask for help in preventing further sabotage.

dictatorship in Europe in deadly pincers.

But just how much was the Mafia involved in the invasion of Sicily? Five days after the landings, an American fighter plane appeared in the sky above Villalba, a small agricultural town in the province of Caltanissetta, halfway between Gela and Palermo, toward which the motorized detachments of the U.S. Seventh Army were headed.[19] From the side of the fuselage fluttered a golden-yellow cloth with a large black letter "L" in the center–the initial letter of "libertà," but also by happy coincidence of "Lucky." That letter "L" was also hoisted on the turret of an armored car that drove up to the gates of Villalba some hours later, for a rendezvous, people say, with Calogero Vizzini, known as Don Calò, one of the most well-known Sicilian mafiosi at the time of the landings,[20] and for whom the Americans had meanwhile dropped an identical piece of cloth. This meeting could have been set up by the intelligence services thanks to the contacts that Luciano had on the island of his birth. Although the story is open to conjecture and may have been embellished, however the facts are interpreted, history suggests this anecdote may have been more than simply wartime folklore.[21]

Powerful Friends At Allied Headquarters

Despite the harsh repression launched by Prefect Cesare Mori during the Fascist period, Don Calogero Vizzini had nonetheless succeeded in exploiting various factors, both to create solid ties to important people in Sicily and later to put himself in a favorable position with the "new" invaders. The export of citrus fruit to the United States had been effectively curtailed by the outbreak of war,[22] bringing to its knees the "Garden" Mafia of Palermo, which had already been hurt in the late nineteenth century by the spread of the phylloxera vine louse that had jeopardized the production of wine. The growing demand for grain and meats from pasturage had, in contrast, raised the net worth of the Mafia families in the island's interior, in particular the family led by Don Calò. Vizzini, put

On July 10, 1943, Anglo-American troops landed in Sicily. It is still debated whether Operation Husky was part of a bargain between the American authorities and the Cosa Nostra.

simply, was someone who mattered, as was evident from his frequent visits to the offices of the Allied Military Government for Occupied Territories (AMGOT*), which was led by Lieutenant Colonel Charles Poletti, the head of the Civil Affairs section of the Seventh Army in charge of western Sicily. Even though Poletti would later declare that "the Mafia is only an intellectual construct" and that "the Allied Military Government never heard it speak,"[23] there is strong evidence that AMGOT and the Allied secret services represented by the Office of Strategic Services (OSS*)—the precursor of the CIA—and the British intelligence service, active above all in the period preceding the landings, were "susceptible" to the influence of organized crime. This can be seen, if from nothing else, by the fact that once the island had been conquered, the Americans entrusted the administration of many towns to various Mafia bosses, including Don Calò, in order to use them as a tool of government.[24] In fact, the Allies were desperate to avoid a situation in which the fall of Fascism, which had meant liberty for Europe, might turn into a revolt favorable to the revolutionary forces of the Left. But in Sicily the "new" invaders could not rely solely on the support of the aristocracy and the landowners,[25] as, say, the British had done in India in order to consolidate their colonial rule. They therefore needed support from the Mafia, with its deep roots in the territory, in order to ensure that the recently liberated cities of Sicily did not end up under the control of the political forces on the Left that were especially active in the countryside.[26]

Prefect Cesare Mori. The Sicilian Mafia was severely damaged during the Fascist period.

Diplomatic Cars and Mafia Interpreters

Other events confirm the existence of, if not an actual criminal pact, then very close relations between the liberating army and Mafia groups. Once again, the scene involved Charles Poletti and AMGOT, which, in Naples in 1944, while the Anglo-American armies were advancing up the Italian peninsula, hired an Italian-American Mafia boss as an interpreter.[27] This was none other than Vito Genovese, who had returned to Naples in 1936 to escape a murder charge. It would later turn out that one of the future bosses of the American Cosa Nostra had used the cover provided by his role in the Allied administration to establish a vast smuggling network in southern Italy, selling foodstuffs stolen from U.S. Army trucks for extremely high prices on the black market.[28] During that period Genovese was praised by his officials for "having reported numerous cases of corruption"[29] and he gave Poletti a 1938 Packard sedan to use during his service with AMGOT. Genovese was in possession of, among other things, a powerful radio transceiver similar to the ones given to spies and infiltrators. He was later

arrested and transferred to New York in order to be tried on the murder charge, but was acquitted in 1946. The only key witness in a position to incriminate him was poisoned while in prison before Genovese's return to the United States.

The Mafia, Cuba, and the Kennedy Assassination

As has been shown, the Mafia has been involved in political affairs on an international level on many occasions. Other members have confessed to involvement on a domestic level, including in the notorious trial of the Italian anarchists, Ferdinando Nicola Sacco and Bartolomeo Vanzetti, found guilty of the murder of a bookkeeper and a security guard at the Slater-Morrill Shoe Company and sent to the electric chair on August 23, 1927, at the Charleston penitentiary. The case was hugely controversial and attracted the attention of many prominent left-wing intellectuals who proclaimed it a miscarriage of justice and continued to campaign long after the sentence was carried out. In his 1973 autobiography, the Italian-American gangster Vincent Teresa disclosed a conversation that he had had with one of the members of the Morelli gang, who admitted committing the crimes for which the two Italians were sentenced to death. "It was me Vinnie, and those two imbeciles got the blame. They were there and we made the most of it; that shows you what justice is."

More recently, the Cosa Nostra has been connected with conspiracy theories surrounding the assassination of President John F. Kennedy in 1963. On November 22 of that year, Kennedy was shot while traveling in a motorcade through downtown

Dallas as part of a two-day goodwill tour of Texas, accompanied by the First Lady, Jackie, and the governor of Texas, John Connally and his wife. At 12:30, a sound like a car backfiring was reported. Kennedy had been shot in the back and throat, and Connally, sitting just in front of the president, seriously wounded. In the confusion that followed Kennedy's driver slowed down and the president received a third shot to the head, destroying most of his brain. The car then sped to the hospital, but the president was declared dead at 1 p.m.

Lee Harvey Oswald was arrested hours later, first and foremost in connection with the murder of a policeman. He was then accused of firing on the president from the window of the School Book Depository overlooking Dealey Plaza. Oswald was charged, although he always maintained he was a "patsy." The following day, as Oswald was transferred from the city to the county jail, local nightclub owner Jack Ruby emerged from the crowd, shooting Oswald in the stomach. He died of his injuries in hospital later that day.

As the nation mourned its president, an official inquiry was set up ten days later by Earl Warren, chief justice of the Supreme Court, to investigate the facts about the assassination. The result—the 888-page Warren Commission Report—was made public in September 1964: it certified that Oswald acted alone and didn't have any accomplices. The report was an attempt to lay to rest many of the theories and conjecture surrounding the president's death, but if anything its sheer size seemed only to add to the extreme confusion surrounding the events. Over the years the forensic details outlined in the report would be analyzed and subject to endless speculation, serving only to fuel suspicions that the assassination was more the fruit of a plot than the work of one sole man; the result of a conspiracy that was being covered up at the highest level.

Conflicting witness accounts and differing interpretations of forensic evidence have caused many to doubt the official report, with one of the most enduring and popular theories being that Oswald was not the only gunman in Dealey Plaza that day, even if it was not possible to identify the other participants in the secret operation, nor to come to any consensus who they might be.[30] Among the various pieces of evidence brought in support of the conspiracy theory is the film shot with an 8 mm camera by Abraham Zapruder, the owner of a clothing manufacturing company, who had come out to cheer the president and ended up filming what was to become the most famous footage of the assassination. The film came into the public eye only five years after the assassination of Kennedy. In the image of the third shot, the president's head is violently thrown backwards, which accredits the theory of a frontal shot and therefore the presence of more than one gunman. However, a detailed examination of the film would show that the head of the president, doubtless stiffened by the lesions caused at the spine by the first projectile, makes an imperceptible movement forwards and then is thrown back. The ejection of cervical matter during the explosion of the cranium would have provoked this backward movement. L. W. Alvarez, winner of the Nobel Prize for physics, who conducted ballistic studies on melons with the same bullets as those used on Kennedy and in similar conditions, demonstrated that this movement happened each time he fired from behind his target. This silent, twenty-six seconds' worth of film provides an almost unimpeded view of the moment of the shooting, but endless speculation and analysis of the film have led many to believe it proves unequivocally that the president was shot from more than one direction. The footage now seems to symbolize what is problematic about any discussion of the president's death: so complex have the conspiracy theories become, that even when evidence seems to support the official version of a single gunman— as a 3-D computerized reconstruction based on the film released in 2003 did[31]—those who disagree claim that the original film was manipulated.

A second official inquest, led by the House Select Committee on Assassination between 1976 and 1979, concluded nevertheless that more than one gunman opened fire on the president, even if it was not possible to determine who organized the assassination. Indeed, several witnesses affirmed

that they heard several gunshots coming from a grassy bank situated at the exit of Dealey Plaza, on Elm Street.

Lee Harvey Oswald, arrested for the assassination of John F. Kennedy. Despite the findings of the Warren Commission Report, which concluded that Oswald acted alone, some have theorized that the orders behind the assassination came from the Cosa Nostra.

Even among those who believe that Oswald was part of a larger conspiracy, acting as a mere footsoldier and taking the fall for more powerful figures, there is no consensus about who might have masterminded the plot. Different theories take suspects as diverse as communist groups, far-right extremists, or the Mafia. Those who believe the Mafia might have been involved look to the organization's interests in Cuba, where, under the protection of the dictator Fulgencio Batista, the Mafia ran a thriving network of casinos as well as prostitution rackets in Havana. Cuba was the place where, in 1947, Lucky Luciano, already in exile in Italy, would have met with local bosses in order to plan the trafficking of narcotics to the United States.

More than ten years later, on January 1, 1959, the triumph of the Fidel Castro's Communist revolution disrupted the bosses' extremely lucrative businesses. It is believed the Mafia became involved in a wide-ranging anti-Castro plot, which culminated in the decision to have Kennedy killed because of his policy of détente and dialogue with the Soviet Union and other Communist countries. According to this theory, the Sicilian-American mafiosi involved in the CIA's attempt to overthrow the Cuban Communist government are the same as those who would later be linked to the murder of the President Kennedy. According to yet another theory—supported, allegedly, by telephone intercepts of conversations between members of the Cosa Nostra—the Mafia was motivated to organize the assassination in order to punish the "betrayal" of an earlier iron-clad agreement between Joseph P. Kennedy, the president's father, and organized crime, to support John F. Kennedy's presidential candidacy. This betrayal supposedly occurred after the election, when the new president and his brother Robert, now attorney general, launched a frontal attack on organized crime with federal prosecutors.[32] All of these theories, even if they couldn't be proven, show in any case the wide presence of the mafia in the collective imagination.

The MAFIA AND POLITICS IN POSTWAR ITALY

The bandit Salvatore Giuliano and the massacre at Portella della Ginestra: the state and the Mafia form an alliance against the Communist advance. The secret pact between the Mafia and state institutions opens the way for big business in contracts. The Corleone families establish themselves. Accusations of government involvement at the highest level. The war against the Mafia escalates.

Bloodshed in Portella della Ginestra

On May 1, 1947, on the plateau of Portella della Ginestra, a resort near the town of Piana degli Albanesi in Palermo, a crowd of peasants—men, women, and children bearing richly decorated handcarts and their livestock—arrived from San Giuseppe Jato and San Cipriello to celebrate May Day. Suddenly, from the rocky cliffs of Monte Pelavet, some several hundred yards from the platform set up for the assembly of Communist Party representatives, a group of commandos, armed with an arsenal of weapons—a .30 caliber Breda heavy machine gun, several Beretta automatic light submachine guns, and some long-range Model 91 rifles—shot into the festive crowd. When they had finished eleven bodies lay dead on the ground, nine adults and two children, along with several wounded, some fatally. From the positions hidden among the rocks, the

Montelepre. This town in the province of Palermo has been notorious for bandits since the early 1800s.

carabinieri would recover at least eight hundred empty cartridges.[1] The meeting, a celebration to mark the victory of the Blocco del Popolo (the Popular Front) in the first elections held in Sicily after World War II, had turned to tragedy.

The news traveled around the world during a sensitive time for Italian politics: the previous year, on June 2, 1946, there had been a referendum over Italy's system of government. The choice was between the monarchy, which had legitimized the Fascist dictatorship during the previous twenty years, and a republic. The majority vote was for the latter; a republic with a constituent assembly charged with drafting a new constitution, which was approved on December 22, 1947. The assembly was dominated by a moderate block represented by the Christian Democrats (with 35.8 percent of the vote), the liberals and republicans (around 11 percent),

and other conservatives, while hard on their heels were the Socialists (20.7 percent) and the Communists (19.97 percent). The scene was watched with concern by the United States, which was engaged in mapping out the future of Europe and in so doing seeking to prevent the advance of communism in countries considered strategic, such as Italy. This was to be accomplished mainly through the Atlantic Alliance, which was set up in opposition to the Soviet Bloc controlled by the U.S.S.R. But in what way was this connected to the massacre? The day immediately after the carnage, the Italian minister of the interior, Mario Scelba, asserted that the event was related to conditions specific to Sicily, and that the slaughter had nothing to do with wider political issues or terrorism. The forces of the Left, for their part, called a general strike and accused the Sicilian landowners of wanting to drown the workers' organizations in blood after the victory of the Blocco del Popolo in the regional elections of 1947. The instigators, in other words, were sought in the shadowy alliance of large agrarian landowners and the Mafia against the renewed demands of the peasantry for a more equitable distribution of land. However, four months after the massacre, a different story emerged: it was proved that the separatist bandit Salvatore Giuliano had given the order to fire on the crowd.

Salvatore Giuliano and the Massacre of Portella della Ginestra

Salvatore Giuliano was born in Montelepre, a town in the eastern part of the hinterlands of Palermo, on November 16, 1922. During World

Left: Comrade or notorious traitor? The bandit Salvatore Giuliano (on the right) and his right-hand man, Gaspare Pisciotta. Many maintain that it was Giuliano's own loyal lieutenant who betrayed him.

Facing page: Giuliano seems to defy the laws of the state in this portrait.

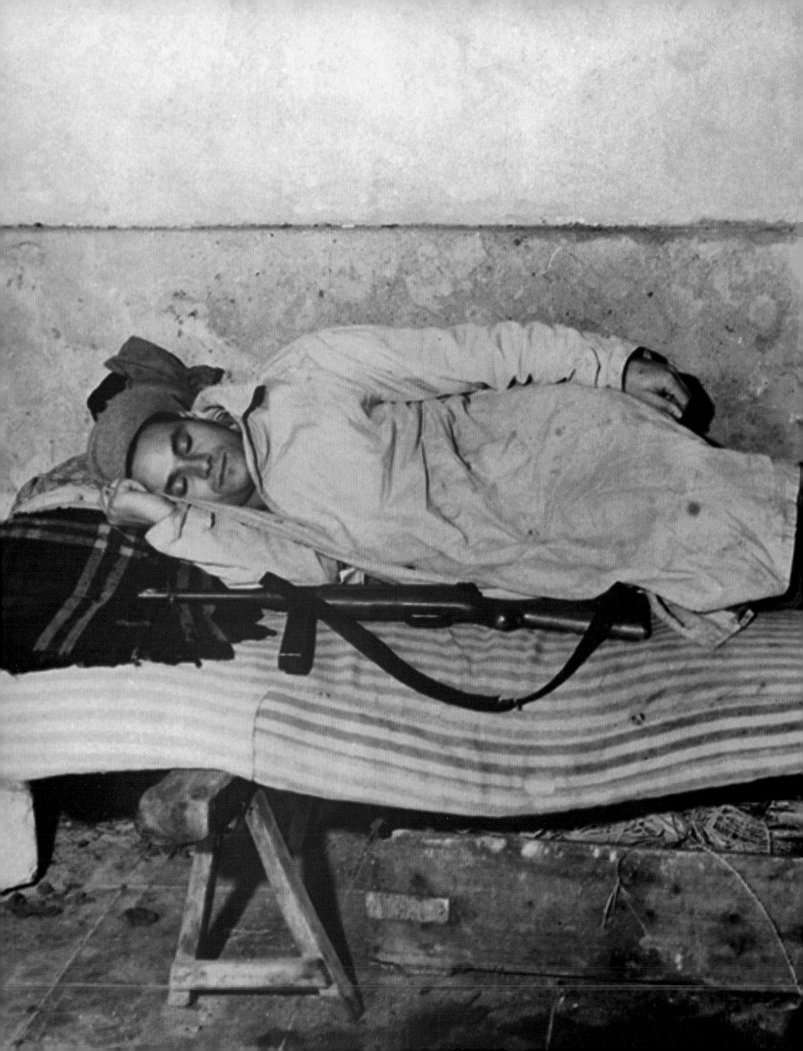

*The King of
Montelepre rests
with an Italian-made
submachine gun
at his side. This was
the weapon used in
the massacre
at Portella della
Ginestra.*

War II he had been a member of the Nazi-Fascist squads that were used to impede the Allied advance after the landings in Sicily.[2] In 1945, after the end of hostilities, Giuliano had assumed command of the Esercito Volontario per l'Indipendenza della Sicilia (Voluntary Army for the Independence of Sicily), an armed paramilitary group belonging to the political movement that advocated Sicily's independence from the central government in Rome. In its early phase it had enjoyed the support of certain important members of the Mafia, who had been employed by the Allied provisional government to maintain order in Sicily and, especially, to oppose the Communists. Despite being neighbors of–and in direct contact with–the Mafia, Giuliano and his men were bandits engaged on two fronts. They carried out terrorist attacks against the carabinieri and the army, in order to further the separatist cause, and they were also involved in a series of illegal activities such as kidnapping. On March 16, 1946, Giuliano and his gang abducted

a rich local landowner and obtained a ransom of 10 million lire, a truly remarkable sum in its day. Of humble origin and uneducated, Giuliano presented himself as a kind of hero who upheld justice and the primacy of Sicily against the oppressive government in Rome, a Robin Hood figure who robbed from the rich and gave to the poor. So what could have motivated him to open fire on the poor in the massacre of Portella della Ginestra? His contradictory behavior after the massacre only seemed to complicate the issue, and was marked both by allegations of important information about the true instigators of the massacre as well as by attempts to limit his responsibility. During a statement to the authorities on April 24, 1950, while on trial for the massacre, along with his lieutenant Gaspare Pisciotta, Giuliano claimed, "I told my men to send fifteen hundred shots into the air to frighten the people at the meeting. I would have taken advantage of the confusion to take the Communist bosses hostage . . . but my men, who were almost all of them just boys, fired on the crowd and then everything that happened."[3]

A few months later, on July 5, 1950, the body of the bandit of Montelepre was found in the courtyard of a house in Castelvetrano in the province of Trapani, Sicily. The official story is that he was killed in a gun battle with the carabinieri, but some sources believe that Giuliano was betrayed, or even assassinated, by his men, and that his dead body was moved to the courtyard in order to make it appear an attempted capture that had come to a bloody ending.

Above left: A procession of Sicilian separatists on a street in Palermo in 1945. At that time, Salvatore Giuliano was in command of an army of volunteers in the Sicilian independence movement.

Facing page: Treason, or massacre secretly organized by the state? The body of Salvatore Giuliano, found riddled with bullets in the courtyard of a house in Castelvetrano on July 5, 1950, as reconstructed in Francesco Rosi's 1961 film, Salvatore Giuliano.

Unknown Leaders of a Shadowy Organization

The trial in Viterbo ended in 1951, with Giuliano and his men found guilty of sole responsibility for the massacre. They were sentenced to life in prison, a verdict that supported the theory put forth by the Ministry of the Interior shortly after the massacre. But the presence of shadowy outside instigators was afterwards confirmed by Gaspare Pisciotta, poisoned in prison with strychnine-laced coffee in 1954 after he made his intentions known to reveal all. It would be left to historians to uncover a motive other than the "mere act of banditry" described during the trial. Many became convinced that the massacre was the first in a long series of episodes connected to the so-called "strategy of tension," a means of curtailing the growth of the Left in Italy and elsewhere. According to this theory, Giuliano was the main protagonist in the first of a chain of bloody events that would leave their mark on the Italian Republic.[4] It had its origins in the

Neo-Fascist Right, and would encompass, among other tragedies, the 1969 massacre at the Piazza Fontana in Milan (seventeen dead and eighty-eight wounded), and the 1980 attack on Bologna train station (eighty-five dead and more than two hundred wounded).

The strategic importance of Sicily and the political importance of both the Communist Party and its Socialist allies had been well known since the time of the Allied landings. A document dated May 16, 1946, drawn up by the Office of Strategic Services (the OSS, the precursor of the CIA) in Italy and now in the National Archives Records Administration (NARA) of the United States in Maryland, contains an intelligence manual for secret propaganda meant to be put into practice in the countries bordering the Mediterranean. One of its chapters described the purpose of the so-called "fake" incident, which was a crime deliberately committed to create a popular reaction and to provide a pretext for the adoption of suitable governmental

countermeasures.[5] The massacres, in other words, were intended to provoke a reaction from the Left, pushing it towards popular insurrection, which would in turn justify violent repression by the authorities as a way to consolidate their own power. According to this version of events, the carnage at Portella della Ginestra served as the dress rehearsal for a new type of political-criminal scenario. In a report prepared in early July 1947, an American secret agent expressed, among others things, the doubt that Giuliano was just a straw man but that, instead, the attacks against the Left were actually probes meant to start a civil war.[6] If there is any truth in this version of events, it is possible that, as can also be seen from British reports available only since 2005, the instigators of the slaughter at Portella della Ginestra were also to be sought on the other side of the ocean, i.e., in a secret institutional network that had the Allied High Command at one end and at the other the X-2*, the counter-espionage service of the OSS. If this were the case, Giuliano was a pawn, manipulated by these forces through the Sicilian Mafia, which had understood that the new winners in Italian politics would not be the Left, but the parties that belonged to the governing coalition, which for many years would be headed by the Christian Democrats.

Gaspare Pisciotta was poisoned in prison after claiming he would reveal the intrigues behind the massacre.

The Mafia Forges a Pact with the Political World

The alliance between the Mafia and the local representatives of the government in Rome grew stronger after the massacre at Portella della Ginestra and became part of a progressive transformation of the criminal organization's economic interests. Starting in the 1950s, under the parallel impetus of an agrarian reform that was considered indispensable by central government in order to respond in even a moderate way to the appeals coming from the peasant class, and of an uncontrolled urbanization that obeyed almost no rules, the foundations were laid for the Mafia's progressive transformation of its interests from the landed estates to the city of Palermo. This was a boom time for reconstruction, as illustrated by vast number of building sites. This phenomenon, seen in the other European nations that had suffered during the war, took place in northwesten Sicily in a very particular way, i.e., through the intermediation of the gangs that controlled the territory, and whose support the politicians could not do without. In 1953 the neighborhoods of Palermo were divided by the Cosa Nostra into thirteen "sectors," each under the control of a different Mafia family,[7] resulting in a further weakening of the presence of the Italian state in Sicily. Over the years, the state's actions became so uncertain and irresolute that the judges and policemen who tried to combat the Mafia became isolated and increasingly powerless to stop the bosses. Because of this many of them were able to remain on the run for decades, despite their identity and illegal activities being public knowledge. An environment of complicity and collusion prevailed, one that, at trial, was able to explain away presence of seemingly irreproachable men amongst the ongoing going violence of car bombs, summary executions, and honor killings.

The "Sack of Palermo" and the Committee of Business Interests

The connection between the Mafia and certain sectors of the political world resulted in a genuine "sacking" of public resources. This phenomenon became known in the history of the Mafia as the "Sack of Palermo." The profits connected to the sharing out of contracts, often to the benefit of the gangs, were managed by an actual committee known as the Comitato d'Affari,[8] or Committee of Business Interests. It was linked to prominent figures in the Christian Democratic party, such as Salvo Lima, who led the municipal administration of Palermo from 1958 until January 1963, and Vito Ciancimino, who was born in Corleone in 1924 and, after having led the Assessorato ai Lavori pubblici (the government office active in the construction sector) from 1959 to 1964, was elected mayor of the city from 1970 to 1971. During the years of great real estate speculation in Palermo, the network of complicity, violence, and criminal activity that was managed by the Comitato d'Affari allowed the Corleonese Mafia to obtain a record number of building permits regularly registered to obliging straw men in collusion with the bosses. Working within this Mafia net of speculative interests were the cousins Ignazio and Nino Salvo, who had obtained from the regional government the right to manage the collection of taxes, retaining for themselves nearly 10 percent of the sums recovered. This flow of money undoubtedly benefited mafiosi and their associates, but it was favorable to the larger economic world as well.

Salvo Lima, mayor of Palermo and a Christian Democrat deputy, was never convicted of any crime but in fact was one of the main figures in the great building speculation that changed the face of the city and enriched the gangs. He was assassinated in 1992 when the Mafia understood that its political contacts could no longer guarantee its protection and impunity.

The political importance of the Mafia continued to grow even during the 1970s, when the reasons for a strategic preoccupation related to the international balance of power and to Italy's membership in the Atlantic Alliance reappeared amid deep concerns over terrorism and the growing influence of the Communist Party. These were the years in which the Cupola* or Commission (i.e., the coordinating body of the various Mafia families), had, to all practical purposes, the upper hand over the Comitato d'affari, which in turn mediated relations between the gangs and corrupt government institutions and became the nerve center for decisions influencing the structure of the city. The conquest of the Commission, which up till then had been under the influence of the Mafia in Palermo, thus became the primary objective of the gangs from the landed estates in Corleone. Led by Totò Riina and Bernardo Provenzano, they launched the final assault on the topmost reaches of the Sicilian Mafia, and also tried to secure absolute control over the market for narcotics. An illustration of the connections between the criminal and political worlds was

Vito Ciancimino, a Christian Democrat and, with Salvo Lima, a main figure in the "Sack of Palermo." He was convicted of associating with the Mafia and other crimes. His revelations about the ties between the Mafia and various official institutions are at the center of judicial inquiries even today.

His power in Italian political life can be surmised by his nickname, "Divo Giulio"—Divine Julius, a reference to Caesar. Among his contacts at the local level, Andreotti numbered mayor of Palermo Salvo Lima as an ally. And yet, from 1979, Andreotti was under investigation for murder and for associating with members of the Mafia, among other offences. On October 23, 1999, he was acquitted with a complete discharge after a three-year trial. In 2002 he was convicted of murder on appeal and sentenced to twenty-four years in prison for the assassination of the Italian journalist, Mino Pecorelli (for political reasons), only to have that ruling overturned in 2003. That year he was also acquitted of any ties with the Mafia, due to a technicality. Although the judges ruled that the crimes were "recognizable in actual fact," for the period preceeding the spring of 1980, Andreotti could no longer be prosecuted because the timing of the crime exceeded the statute of limitations. The verdict was upheld by the Italian Court of Cassation on October 15, 2004, but Andreotti remains acquitted of all charges due to the timing of the crimes.

provided by Antonio Calderone, a contractor belonging to the Mafia in Catania who decided to cooperate with the authorities in 1986 after his gang had been badly hit by rivals. "The men in politics are always looking for us, because we control many, very many, votes. In order to have an idea of how much the Mafia can mean in an election . . . consider that every man of honor, between friends and relatives, can deliver more than forty to fifty people. In the province of Palermo there are between fifteen hundred and two thousand men of honor*. . . . Multiply by fifty and you have a nice bundle of seventy-five to one hundred thousand votes that you can send to the parties and candidates who are your friends."[9]

Accusations of Complicity at the Highest Levels of Government

This web of collusion extended to the most prominent figures in Italian politics. Among them was Giulio Andreotti, a leader of the Christian Democrats who, starting in the postwar period, would occupy the most prestigious government positions, including that of prime minister, defense minister, and minister of the interior.

The Winds of Change

During the 1980s, attacks by the Mafia on the judges, policemen, and politicians who tried to curb their power became more intense. Among those who fell foul of the gangs were Piersanti Mattarella, then president of Sicily, who sought to impose order on the region, and then parliamentary deputy Pio La Torre, who had proposed a law making Mafia conspiracy a crime. This was significant in the ongoing battle against

organized crime in that it permitted, among other things the confiscation of Mafia-owned property. La Torre paid for the legislation with his life, when he and his driver were murdered by the Mafia in their car as they approached Communist Party headquarters.

But it would take a second act of violence for La Torre's law to be approved by the Italian parliament on December 13, 1982. General Carlo Alberto Dalla Chiesa, appointed after La Torre's death as prefect in Palermo to continue the fight against Mafia power, was shot on Via Carini in Palermo on September 3, 1982 with his young wife, Emanuela Setti Carraro.[10] The barrage of Kalashnikov bullets also ended the life of Dalla Chiesa's bodyguard, Domenico Russo, at the wheel of the escort car. This hail of bullets ended the first one hundred days on the job for the new prefect. But this was in fact the third time Dalla Chiesa had returned to Sicily, during a career which took in the fight against banditry of the immediate postwar period, and during which he had put Luciano Leggio behind bars for the murder of the trade union leader Placido Rizzotto. Over the course of those one hundred days as prefect Dalla Chiesa had fought in vain for the special powers promised by the government in Rome to launch a counteroffensive against the Mafia.

The 1980s were also the years of the Palermo "Spring," which saw the spontaneous reaction on the part of honest Sicily against organized crime, and which imparted a burst of new energy to the activities of the judges and investigators in the first line of battle with the Mafia. It would

Right: The fight against the Mafia in Sicily. General Carlo Alberto Dalla Chiesa (last figure on the left) and the Procuratore of Palermo, Cesare Terranova (in the center, with eyeglasses), in the course of an investigation in Marsala. Both were murdered by the Mafia.

Facing page: Giulio Andreotti in 1954, when he was undersecretary to the president of the Council of Ministers. Indicted on charges of complicity with the Mafia, he was acquitted by the Italian Court of Cassation in 2003.

take the end of the Cold War for the central government in Rome to take the same stand. In order to understand clearly the considerable power of the ever more effective laws against organized crime, one must follow, with its striking chronological coincidences, the path of those geopolitical transformations that followed the fall of the Berlin Wall. In 1986 saw the introduction of severe prison sentences for those convicted of Mafia-related crimes in Italy, including solitary confinement in maximum-security prisons with

no possibility of contact with the outside world. The aim was to eliminate any channels by which Mafia bosses could issue instructions from inside their cells to be carried out in the outside world, such as death sentences. In 1991, an organization known as the Direzione Investigativa anti-Mafia was established to coordinate the exchange of information between the carabinieri, the local police, and the Guardia di Finanza, a military police force under direction of the Ministry of Economy and Finance. A year later, the Direzione Nazionale anti-Mafia was established, a kind of "super public prosecutor's office" that facilitated, among other things, a greater degree of cooperation in the work of the judges and a more efficient exchange of information between them.[11]

White-Collar Lawlessness and the End of the Corleonesi

By the 1990s even the Mafia recognized the tide had turned irreversibly. But nevertheless, the organization punished those political friends no longer able to guarantee impunity in exchange for the electoral support of the gangs, as seen, for example, by the murder of Salvo Lima on March 16, 1992. Equally, the Mafia targeted white-collar workers (such as Ignazio Salvo, murdered on September 17, 1992) who had made their fortunes through shady business deals. There then followed an attempt by the Mafia to carry out its own "strategy of tension," through blackmailing the government by putting it under the spotlight of public opinion. On May 27, 1993, the Corleonesi placed a car bomb with more than five hundred pounds of explosives on Via

dei Georgofili in Florence, just two steps from the Uffizi, one of the country's most important museums. Five people were killed and the nearby Torre dei Pulci collapsed, with damage to some of the works of art housed in the museum. Later that year, two bombs exploded in Rome, one near the basilica of San Giovanni in Laterano and the other near the Church of San Giorgio al Velabro. But the destruction had the opposite effect to the one intended by the Mafia and did not galvanize public opinion against the government. However, it did drive some of those who had collaborated with the authorities to jump ship, leaving the Corleonesi adrift and minus some of their members following a series of very public arrests.

Behind the Scenes of the Massacres

But could the massacres of 1993 be attributed solely to the Mafia's violent reaction to the winds of change blowing ever more strongly against them, or were they a further punitive reaction against something that ran much deeper?

Facing page:
State tax collectors and men of honor. Ignazio Salvo (pictured) managed the tax system in Sicily for the government along with his cousin Nino.

Attacks and massacres carried out against art. The devastating effects of the Mafia's violent reaction against the state even damaged monuments in Rome. Above, from left to right: Rubble of the church of San Giorgio al Velabro, near the Arco di Giano; investigation of the scene of the explosion (which produced no casualties as opposed to that of Florence); the damaged church façade.

In 2009, Massimo Ciancimino, son of Vito, the former mayor of Palermo who died in 2002, made some disturbing allegations about the activities committed during that time. According to Massimo, the secrets of those tragic years were contained on a single sheet of paper, delivered to the judicial authorities and which testified to the existence of a bargain between the Corleonesi and the government to end the violence and bombings. It spelled out twelve demands as the price the government would have to pay to secure peace. These included, among other things, the abolition of the crime of belonging to a Mafia organization, recourse to the European Court of Justice in order to amend the results of the maxi-trial against the Mafia, and a reform of the justice system to make it similar to that in the United States, with greater guarantees for the accused. Attached to the list was a second sheet written by the former mayor of Palermo with the proposed modifications to the twelve items requested by the Corleonesi. Pasted to it was a Post-it note on which Ciancimino had written "consigned" to a colonel in the special operations division of the carabinieri. Was this the umpteenth orchestrated attempt to discredit the government, or was it concrete proof that the Italian state had entered into negotiations with the Mafia?[12] The final word on this subject remains to be written.

BOSSES,
GODFATHERS, AND WOMEN
IN THE MAFIA

*Portraits of godfathers past and present, from Don
Calogero Vizzini to Frank Coppola and Gaetano
Badalamenti. Bloody mob wars and the struggle
for control of the whole organization. The expansion
of the drug trade. The search for the Capo dei Capi.
Luciano Leggio and the unstoppable rise of the Corleone
gang in Sicily. The Mafia wars and attempts at peace.
The role and power of women in the clans of southern Italy.*

A Don's Career

World War II had only recently ended, but
in Villaba, a village set among the estates of
Caltanissetta, where Don Calogero Vizzini was
born on July 24, 1887, it was as though time
has stood still. He conducted his business in
the village in his shirtsleeves, jacket on his arm,
a cigar always in his mouth. He wore a wide-
brimmed hat, his eyes hidden by large tortoise-
shell glasses.[1] He was called "Don," out of respect,
like the Spanish noblemen who ruled Sicily
during the time of the Bourbons in the eighteenth
century.[2] The people of his village greeted him
and kissed his hands, as was customary during

the Middle Ages when vassals were required to
pay their respects to the lords of large landed
estates. In the twentieth century, customs of a
bygone day continued.

Don Calò was much more than a mayor. He
was a man of honor—the term used by mafiosi
to describe important figures amongst them—and
a friend of the Americans who wiped out the
Fascists. Fascists were enemies of the Mafia, and
besides, the Mafia is always on the side of the
winners. Don Calò was also much more than a
boss. No one would have dreamt of taking him
for just the local village mafioso. For most people
he was, simply put, someone who "arranges

*Don Calogero Vizzini,
the godfather of
Villalba. This mayor
of the rural Mafia had
powerful friends
in the government
in Palermo.*

things."[3] If a local businessman needed to hire someone, he only needed to go to Don Calò. If one lacked the high school diploma required for a particular job, he was always the one to help, as an educational qualification could be obtained in exchange for other favors.[4] Before an election, politicians might be obliged to bargain for their preferences with Don Calò—votes could be secured in exchange for other services, and cooperation with Don Calò ensured the correct results. Even businessmen went to him when they needed help with the banks; Don Calò had influence with the banks because he was on good relations with the clergy, and the banks could not risk the displeasure of the high prelates of the Church. Both bank and church were united in their fear of any change to the established order in the countryside, with its ever-present threat of workers' solidarity and Communist agitation.[5]

But Vizzini's motives were by no means altruistic. He began his "career" as a *campiere*, or armed guard, in the service of a boss on a landed estate. He protected the peasants from assault and theft by bandits, and at the same time was involved in the illegal business of trafficking horses commandeered by the army in the countryside. Even diseased animals commanded a high price, while the very best ones remained with their legitimate owners, thanks to the "protection" of Don Calò—and always, of course, in exchange for other favors. Vizzini represented an "old" Mafia, one which was capable, on the one hand, of mediating disputes between families in order to avoid useless bloodshed over territory and, on the other, of corrupting official institutions in order to

assure the freedom for the organization to develop its illegal trafficking.

A Mafia "Gentleman"

Thanks to the wealth he accumulated, and his extensive network of accomplices, Don Calò was able to become a tax collector. He rented land and, when necessary, managed to evade justice, thanks to powerful supporters. He acquired at public auction an estate of some twelve hundred acres in the area of Serradifalco, but it was with the landing in Sicily of the American and British armies that his influence really grew. The Allies needed to establish order on the island and, above all, to avoid a situation in which the fall of Fascism might also bring about a revolt favorable to the revolutionary forces of the Left. But, unlike the English in India, the new invaders of Sicily could not count on the support of the aristocracy and landowners.[6] They had to deal with the Mafia and with men of honor such as Don Calò, who had a

Above left: Funeral eulogy for a man of honor. The cloth that was attached to the door of the church on the day of Don Calò's funeral can be seen in the photo. On the saint's cards that were distributed to relatives and friends the words "la sua mafia fu amore" ("his Mafia was love") were written.

Facing page: The funeral for a "state within the state." The coffin of Don Calò carried on the shoulders of his fellow villagers.

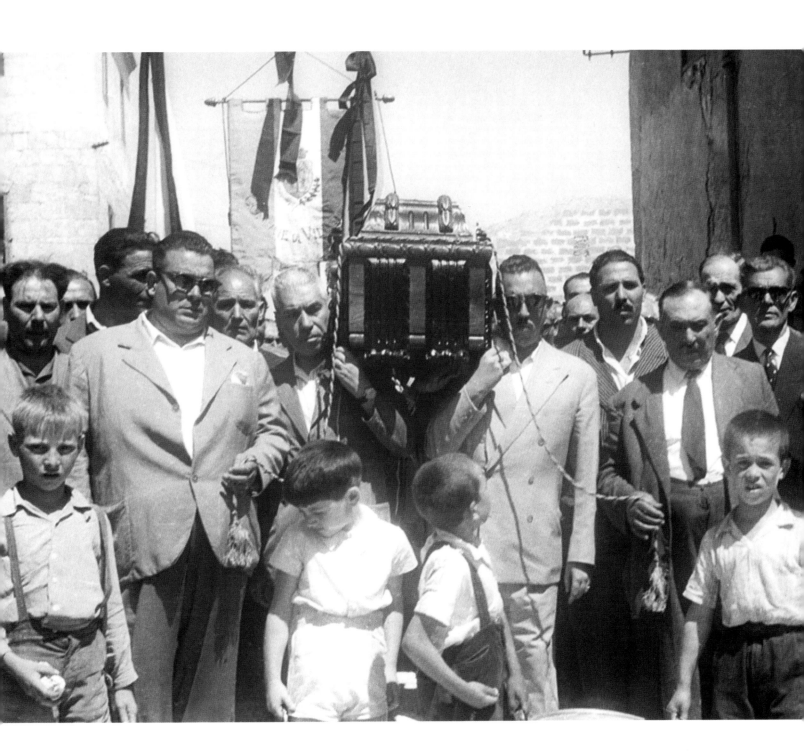

COPPOLA FRANC. PAOLO

FU FRANCESCO

decisive role in the control of the territory. Because of this, the Allied provisional military government came to rely on men like Don Calò, and also on advice from the higher-ups in the Sicilian Catholic Church. Equally importantly, Don Calò knew his way around the political circles of Palermo. And like the other mafiosi, he could fully exploit the cover provided by the Allies as a way to reinforce the power of organized crime on the island. He would, for example, make criminal investigation files disappear from the records offices of the law courts of Caltanissetta. When the Allied administration took over its operations, he would loot the warehouses of the agrarian cooperative and the barracks abandoned by the fleeing Italian army. Food, clothing, and motor vehicles were resold on the black market, and the Mafia began to breathe again after its repression by the Fascists.

In the town of Villalba, the power of Don Calò's gang was unlimited. They owned land, they controlled the bank that lent money to farmers, and they were in charge of public works. Everything was in the hands of one family.[7] With regard to the Americans, Don Calò and the other bosses such as Giuseppe Genco Russo played their role to perfection: they complained about being victims of Fascism and, in the climate of political chaos in Sicily at the time, they sided with the Movement for the Independence of Sicily (MIS*), a group made up of conservative aristocrats and landowners who wanted a Republic of Sicily separate from the rest of Italy. In Palermo in December 1943, the MIS distributed thousands of badges bearing the number "49", symbolizing one star to be added to the forty-eight that at the time were on

Frank "Three Fingers" Coppola. It is said that his hand was caught in a safe. Whether true or not, the mutilation did not keep him from managing the drug traffic between Italy and the United States.

the American flag.[8] But for Vizzini and the other bosses, their interest in the separatist movement was only temporary, intended to reassure the Allied government about their commitment to combat the threat of Communism. In 1948 Don Calò and other Sicilian mafiosi abandoned the MIS and openly sided with the Christian Democrat Party. For the next fifty years, the party[9] would guarantee that Italy remain part of the Atlantic Alliance, opposed to the bloc formed by the former Soviet Union and its satellite countries.

Between 1943 and 1946 Vizzini and his cohorts laid the foundations for the international gangsterism developed in America by "Lucky" Luciano. A great wave of drugs and dollars, followed by a river of blood, would flow along the criminal route that linked the two worlds. And yet, at Don Calò's funeral on 11 July, 1954, an eloquent eulogy was hung on the door of the church of Villalba. It celebrated "a man who was wise, dynamic, and tireless," able to provide "comfort to the workers" in the sulfur mines; a man who labored "always for the good," and earned "a reputation highly esteemed in Italy and elsewhere." Don Calò was "great because of the persecutions he suffered, and greater still because of his misfortunes," and was referred to by "all his friends" and "by his former adversaries" as "the finest; a gentleman."[10] The commemorative portrait (known as a *santino*) that was distributed in his memory showed him in a jacket and necktie, embellished with phrases even more effusive than those on the church door. "Enemy of all injustices, humble among the meek, and great among the greatest, he showed by his words, and by his works, that his Mafia was not criminal, that it was, with regard to the law, a defender of every right, with a greatness of spirit," and, more than anything else, "with love."[11]

The Expansion of the Narcotics Trade

The emergence of the Mafia outside the borders of Sicily in the postwar period and the strengthening of ties with the Sicilian families in the United States went hand in hand with the increase in the traffic in drugs. The market for drugs required an expansion of the organization's territories, involving the constant movement of people from one side of the ocean to the other, in addition to the creation of "operational centers" in areas outside Sicily.[12] Like Lucky Luciano, who was freed from prison and deported from the United States in 1946, in recognition of the "valuable services" performed for the Allies when they landed in 1943, Frank "Three Fingers" Coppola was also forced to return to Italy immediately after the end of the war. He was born in 1891 in Partinico, Sicily, and emigrated to the United States in 1926 to escape the forced residence imposed on him during the Fascist repression. On his return to Sicily, Coppola brought back all the connections and knowledge that he had acquired as the Cosa Nostra's main contact in Kansas City.

Coppola had been one of the leaders of the trade in narcotics since its earliest days. From his base in Anzio, on the outskirts of Rome, he built a network that would reach the north of Italy and eventually serve "branch offices" in the United States and other parts of Europe. It would also push the Sicilian-American Mafia in the direction of a new model that would make ever greater use of

armed force in order to control criminal activities worth unprecedented billions. Coppola's troubles with the authorities did not prevent his receiving a hero's welcome in his native land, with music and flags as if for a national holiday, nor the gift of an honorary card by the Federazione Universitaria Cattolica Italiana as a "benefactor of orphans and of the church of Partinico."[13]

In Search of the *Capo dei Capi* of the Cosa Nostra

This complex web of relationships and connections between the Old World and the New would cause the United States to experience a rude awakening. By the 1950s the American authorities had begun to suspect that the Mafia had become "a government within the government, secret and international," with a "board of directors and its chiefs for each country and region in which it operates, the United States included."[14] It also had a new position, one that had never existed before, the *Capo dei Capi* *("Boss of Bosses") in command of an "octopus" (*piovra*, another name for the Mafia) with branches in many countries.[15]

The mysteries that surround the Mafia underworld have helped feed the myth that they can strike with utmost precision at the highest levels (leading even, as has been seen earlier, to the theory that the Mafia were responsible for the assassination of President John F. Kennedy).[16] Certainly figures such as Luciano and Coppola used every possible means to control the international traffic in drugs. The trade in citrus fruits and other local goods—olive oil, cheese, fruit, coffee, sardines, and anchovies—between

Fugitives–in a manner of speaking. Luciano Leggio began his career as a campiere and became head of the Corleone clan. Evading capture for many years, he was protected by a combination of omertà and high-level cover-up that gave him the freedom of movement necessary to watch over the interests of the Mafia.

Italy and the United States was the perfect means of transporting morphine acquired under-the-counter from pharmaceutical companies in the north of Italy as well as opium from poppy fields in the Far East. In New York, companies specializing in the import of such foodstuffs, such as the Mamma Mia Oil Company, were in the hands of Sicilian-American mafiosi.[17] But the idea of using the trade in foodstuffs to supply drugs to the rich American market was not new: by the early 1900s shipments of cheese from Sicily to the United States were already being used to smuggle contraband watches and jewels hidden inside properly declared merchandise. Drugs were much lighter than such goods and it was simple enough to hide them in envelopes placed inside cheese, for example. (Once the crust had formed, it was virtually impossible to find the illegal cargo, and neither the consistency nor the weight of the product changed.[18])But drugs also traveled by other means, such as in gift parcels entrusted to emigrants for relatives living in America.

The American Cosa Nostra and the Sicilian Mafia did not only have an exclusive copyright on illegal methods of transport: they managed the traffic by long distance and controlled almost the

on the model of the crime syndicate in the United States, a coordinating "commission" that would prevent any breakdown in an already delicate equilibrium and the outbreak of a devastating war between the families for control of ever larger parts of the drugs market.

Luciano Leggio Destroys the Link between New World Mafia and Old

Smashing that equilibrium imposed by the "old" gangs was the idea of Luciano Leggio (sometimes spelled "Liggio" on court documents), born in Corleone on May 6, 1925. At the end of World War II, the boss who would go on to take the Corleonesi to the uppermost reaches of the Sicilian Mafia was little more than a petty thief, albeit one who was ruthless and preternaturally skilled with a handgun. Livestock theft was his chosen career, and he quickly became rich thanks to illegal trafficking in animals resold on the meat market in Palermo. Leggio became the right-hand man of Michele Navarra, the boss of a gang known as the Mafia of the Gardens of the Conca d'Oro ("the Golden Conch," a stretch of coastline outside Palermo). Navarra was known by the Sicilian nickname of *u patri nostri* ("Our Father"). Nominally an insurance company doctor, he was in fact the uncontested godfather of the hinterlands of Palermo, where the crime families controlled the water wells and would blackmail the owners of the citrus orchards by threatening to leave them dry. Navarra was a ferocious man of honor, but, according to Leggio, he had no foresight and did not see the potential in new lines of business such as public contracts or the drug trade.

Left: The automobile riddled with bullets in which Michele Navarra, a medical doctor and the boss of Corleone, was traveling with a colleague. Leggio had decided to eliminate Navarra, who succeeded in getting out of the car but was followed and killed a short way off.

Facing page: Wanted by the police, in permanent hiding. Among these police photos distributed in the early 1960s is that of a young Bernardo Provenzano.

entire territory in which the criminal enterprise was conducted. The "trademark" of their business was that they did not fear rivals. They were able to punish anyone who might attempt to cheat them and because of this all transactions were carried out strictly on a verbal basis, without any written contract. They made use of an extensive sales network as well as of huge amounts of risk capital, because they were always in danger of being discovered. In the 1950s, quite apart from the cost of the drugs, the cost of one ship used in narcotics traffic could reach forty thousand dollars per voyage, to cover charges for chartering the ship, wages for the crew, and rent of sophisticated telecommunications equipment. It is no wonder that the bosses of the American Cosa Nostra decided to meet with their Sicilian "cousins" at the Palms Hotel in Palermo, from October 12–16, 1957, in order to decide how to divide the richest pie ever prepared by the criminal organization. Their intent was to persuade the Sicilians to create,

MURATORE BERNARDO   PROVENZANO SALVATORE   DI PUMA ANGELO   DI PUMA BIAGIO

MACALUSO GIOVANNI   PROVENZANO SIMONE   CAMMARATA FRANCESCO

RUFFINO GIUSEPPE   PROVENZANO BERNARDO   BAGARELLA CALOGERO

DOMARA VINCENZO   GENNARO FILIPPO   MANGIAMELI ANTONINO

For example, Navarra was opposed to a dam in the Valle del Belice that, carrying water to the Conca d'Oro, would have broken the monopoly on the distribution of water that the Mafia families had controlled for decades.[19]

Leggio, who in the meantime had become the owner of a transport company, was in favor of the project, and of the public financing that could be rigged to the Mafia's benefit.[20] He and the Corleonesi found new allies in a branch of the Greco family dominant in Villalba, in the Palermo hinterlands, and led by Michele Greco, "il Papa". Navarra's final hour had come. On the evening of August 2, 1958, a hail of bullets showered Michele Navarra's Fiat as he drove home with a colleague. One hundred and twelve machine gun bullets stopped him forever, and opened the way for the tyrannical rise of Leggio and the Corleonesi to the highest levels of the Sicilian Mafia.

This place would one day be occupied by Totò Riina and his son-in-law Leoluca Bagarella, and by Bernardo Provenzano. They all came from the same rural area in the heart of Palermo and would exercise influence over the fortunes of the entire organization up to the present day. For instance, when the first Mafia war broke out in 1962, it was ostensibly triggered by a missing payment for a shipment of heroin sent to the United States, but at its heart was a much larger issue to do with power. At stake was not only control of the narcotics traffic, which would experience an unprecedented boom up until the end of the 1970s, but also the division of parts of Palermo suitable for property development.[21] Leggio and the Greco family were not content to limit themselves with second-tier

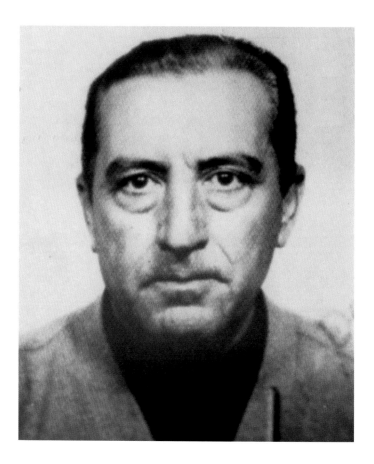

activities such as contraband; they turned their attention to areas of the city where property speculation was running wild and were prepared to wipe out anyone who presented an obstacle to their new ambitions. This included the Barbera family, which, at this time claimed exclusive control over the city's cement rackets.

The Godfathers at War

Totò Riina would much later say that in order to make peace one must make war. In this way, the Mafia in Palermo would, soon after the first large-scale battle in its history, reorganize on one side around Michele Greco and Stefano Bontate, head of the Santa Maria di Gesù family, and both from well-known families in the outskirts of Palermo, and on the other around the more free-

Michele Greco, known as "il Papa," was among those who tried, without success, to oppose the violent rise to power of the gangs from Corleone.

Don Tano Badalamenti. After emigrating to the United States, he returned to Sicily and became head of the Sicilian Mafia. He was posato (Mafia slang that means forced to leave a position) from the powerful Corleone clan.

wheeling Corleonesi from the countryside, under the command of Leggio. (The former right-hand man of Michele Navarra escaped the law for years, and was sentenced for his murder only in 1970, but evaded capture until 1974.) By this time, the profits generated by the drug trade were astronomical. The methods of production and distribution had been perfected thanks to support from associates in Marseille—the so-called French Connection*, which included figures such as Albert Bergamelli and Jacques Berenguer—who refined, in France, heroin from both the Near and Far East that was later sold by the Sicilians to buyers from the United States. This elaborate network extended even to Rome, where Pippo Calò, the "treasurer" of the Sicilian Mafia, tried to increase the illegal traffic in drugs by employing the fearsome Magliana gang[22]

(notorious in the 1970s and 1980s for committing a series of shocking murders in Rome). However, pressure from the FBI and from Italian and French investigators on its connections in France persuaded the Mafia to make more refinements to its methods of exploiting the narcotics traffic.

The Useless Peace of Don Tano Badalamenti

Gaetano Badalamenti reached the top levels of the Sicilian Mafia in 1975. Born in 1923, he left his hometown of Cinisi, Sicily, in 1946 and settled in Detroit, remaining in the United States until 1950 when the American authorities deported him to Italy. Together with Stefano Bontate and the Corleonesi (now led by Totò Riina following Leggio's life sentence), Don "Tano" tried, among other things, to guarantee the peace between the families in Italy, through his many contacts in the United States. It was a peace that served to facilitate the continuing drug trade centered around Sicily, although certain things had changed compared to earlier years. Now, although the importing might be done with the help of experts from Marseille, the Sicilians refined the heroin themselves. This demanded a new position: someone to acquire the raw material in the Far East in order to sell it to the refinery, which assumed the risk of managing the cargo while it was being processed. This person would then buy the processed drugs back from the refinery as "finished goods" for sale in the United States, creating a veritable tidal wave of dollars headed back to Italy (almost 1 billion dollars a year until the end of the 1970s) to be split among the partners who had financed the initial purchase.

This position was occupied by the "third Mafia"[23] that connected the Old World with the New, and of which Gaetano Badalamenti was a part. And it was the question of control over these profits that sparked off the "Second Mafia War" in Palermo. That war was preceded by the bloodless removal of Don Tano by the ruling Commission of the Sicilian Mafia as carried out by the Corleonesi and Michele Greco. It began on April 30, 1981, with the murder of Stefano Bontate by the Corleonesi to enable them to consolidate their leadership of the organization. The battle would take more than five hundred lives in scarcely two years, a blood sacrifice that would weigh heavily on fifty-four families and more than three thousand associates in every part of Palermo and its outlying districts.

The new system for the production and sale of drugs gave rise in Palermo to the so-called Pizza Connection, which made use of pizzerias in New York for illicit drug dealing. That same system would cause Gaetano Badalamenti to be extradited to the United States in 1984, where he was the principal defendant in the criminal case brought by U.S. District Attorney Rudolph Giuliani against the American Cosa Nostra. Badalamenti's defense lawyer tried to minimize the sentence and obtain leniency from the jury, making an appeal to the old-fashioned and patriotic "Mafia ways" of a simple smuggler. ("To defend the honor of the Sicilian family one does not turn to the authorities. In Sicily, if someone has a problem, he takes care of it himself."[24]) But the lawyer's words fell on deaf ears and Badalamenti earned forty-five years in prison.

The Rise and Fall of the *Capo dei Capi*

During the mid-1980s the ruthless and bloody "new Mafia" of the drug traffickers would bury, under a mountain of cadavers, the last vestiges of the old-style godfathers. The main protagonist in this season of terror was Salvatore "Toto" Riina, known as Totò u' curtu ("Totò the Dwarf") because of his short stature. Born in Corleone on November 16, 1930, during his youth he stole from and extorted the local peasants, until he became the right-hand man of Luciano Leggio, along with fellow local Bernardo Provenzano. After Leggio's arrest in 1974, Riina would lead the Corleonesi in their conquest of Palermo and the profitable markets in drugs and public contracts. A sinister and charismatic figure in this "new Mafia," Riina would eliminate every one of his rivals in the Commission to become the Capo dei Capi of the Sicilian Mafia. Riina resorted to unprecedented levels of violence, even against representatives of the state such as the policemen, carabinieri, and judges who tried to stop the surging waves of violent crime. He was responsible for the assassinations of the prosecutors Giovanni Falcone and Paolo Borsellino in two separate car bomb attacks in 1992. Riina was convinced that these massacres would force the government to negotiate with the Mafia, and that the murderous mix of criminal underworld and official "upper world" would prevail once more, but he was mistaken. After years of indecision and collusion with the Mafia, the Italian state had finally decided to turn over a new leaf. Perhaps it was because, with the fall of communism, there was

Totò Riina was arrested after twenty-four years on the run, following an operation carried out by special detachments of the carabinieri. The way in which he came to be arrested, and the failure to search his villa promptly after the arrest, are still questioned today.

Left: Giuseppa Vitale, known as Giusi or Giusy, was a gruesome but clear example of women's emancipation in the world of organized crime. She later cooperated with the authorities.

Facing page: Indomitable women: Maria Filippa Messina was the first woman sentenced to "hard time" in prison, something reserved for those found guilty of Mafia-related crimes.

no longer any need to collude with the criminal gangs in exchange for the votes they controlled, and which had been a way to guarantee elections for a government that wanted to keep Italy in an Atlantic Alliance opposed to the Soviet bloc. Riina was arrested in Palermo on January 15, 1993, after almost twenty-four years on the run, possibly betrayed by his own "heir apparent," Provenzano, to whom the scepter of the Mafia was now given. In order to guarantee the survival of the organization, however, this new Capo dei Capi was forced to adopt a new strategy: one in which the Mafia was once again invisible to the eyes of the state. Despite this, he was arrested on April 11, 2006, in the same town of Corleone where he had been "hiding" for forty-three years, protected by the local code of silence.

Women of the Mafia

Women have usually played a secondary role in the Sicilian Mafia, as they generally do in the patriarchal social systems typical of southern Italy, although recently there have been instances in which women have become the leaders of their clans. When men assume the responsibility of command, their oath of loyalty to the Mafia allows them to go outside the bonds of family to give priority to the needs of the organization. Mafia women have traditionally been wives and mothers first and foremost, yet that role has begun to change.

Giusy Vitale is one of the most striking examples of this new Mafia woman. Before going over to the authorities in February 2005, she was the first female boss in the Sicilian Mafia. In 1998 she controlled the area of Partinico, on the outskirts

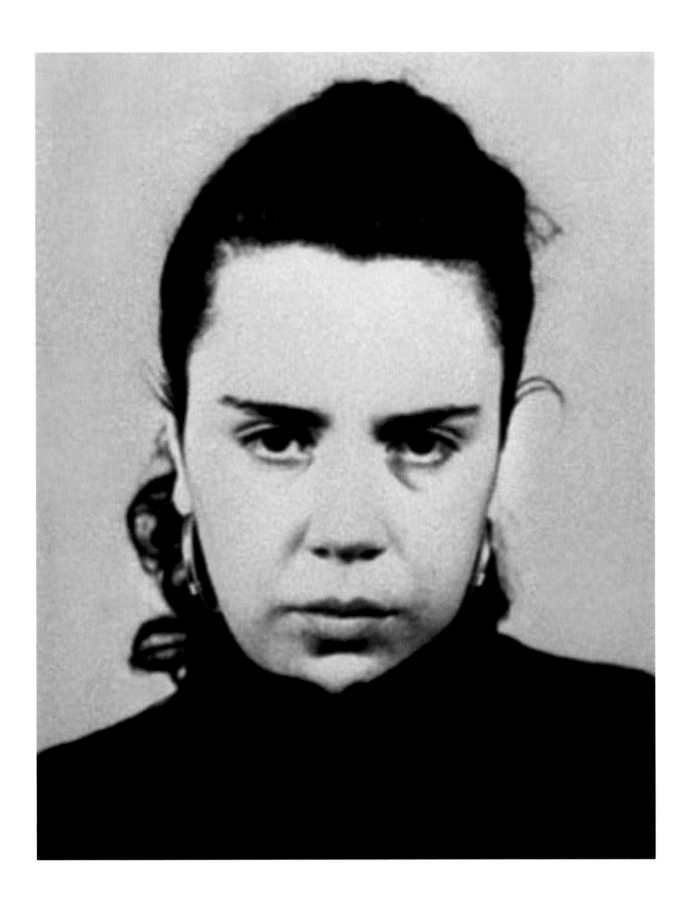

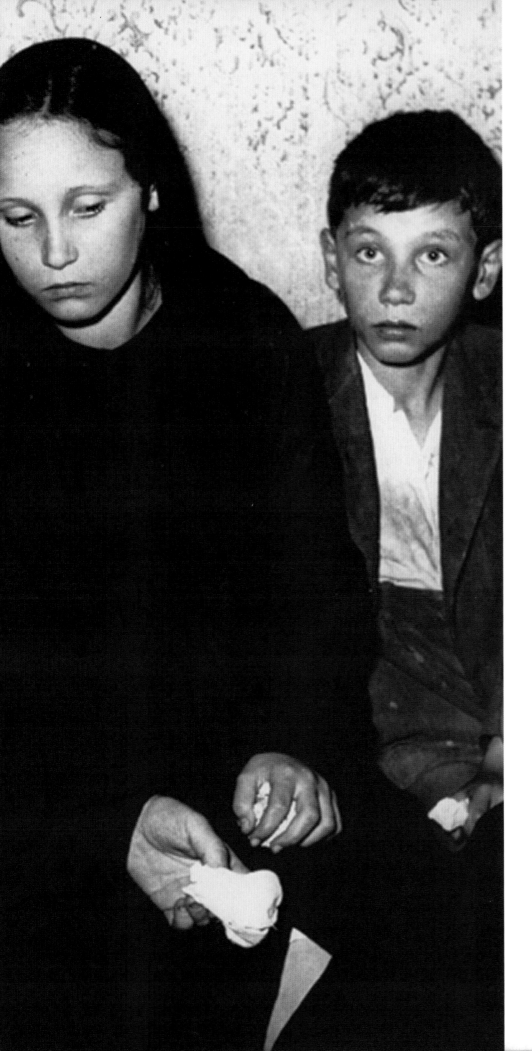

*Grief
in a Sicilian family.*

of Palermo, "with the firm hand of a godfather," and was involved in extortion rackets, real estate speculation, money laundering*, and drug trafficking.[25] It was she who told of having met Bernardo Provenzano, the last of the Mafia bosses, traveling undisturbed around Italy dressed like a bishop to escape a nationwide police hunt.

Other female Mafia figures include Maria Filippa Messina. Detained for associating with the Mafia, she was the first woman in Italy to be sentenced to a maximum-security prison, without visitors or any communication with the outside world, as per Article 41a of the Italian penal code, reserved for those charged with Mafia-related crimes. Serafina Battaglia Leale's association with the Mafia, on the other hand, led ultimately to her cooperation with the authorities. Her husband had been killed by a rival gang in 1960, followed two years later by her son, even though she had sought protection from one of the Mafia bosses. But it was no use: the life of the Leale family's son had already been "sold" to a rival family and the person entrusted with defending him was the one who would shoot him in the back. For Serafina it was the ultimate betrayal, and she didn't hesitate to tell the authorities everything she knew.

Women also play a part in the Camorra, the criminal organization that controls Naples. Although modeled on the Sicilian Mafia it lacks its pyramidal structure and is composed instead of rival clans in conflict with one another.[26] Within the clans, when necessary, women are authorized to exercise the same powers as men to avenge themselves for wrongs suffered. Pupetta Maresca was one such example. On October 4, 1955, while pregnant, she confronted the suspected assassin of her husband Pasquale Simonetti, and killed him with a pistol. Pasquale had been murdered the preceding summer during one of the never-ending struggles for territory between gangs.[27]

Today the female heirs of Pupetta Maresca belong to a criminal geography that has changed greatly. The most daring and most battle-hardened of them run the gangs in place of their husbands when they are sent off to jail, and it is not uncommon for a woman to refuse to relinquish that power afterwards. For this reason, criminal investigations increasingly lead to the mass arrest of Camorra women. Meanwhile the *guaglioni** (dialect for "boys"), or soldiers, of this criminal army remain behind to watch over them, with a mixture of astonishment and admiration.

In Calabria, the undisputed realm of the 'Ndragheta, women perform the tasks traditionally allotted to them by a patriarchy. The 'Ndragheta's strength lies not only in its capacity to branch out internationally, but also in a structure that is much more closed than that of the Sicilian Mafia, and is therefore resistant to infiltration by outside families. For this reason the role of the 'Ndrangheta's women is to uphold the values of the clan, its secrets bound by the *sorella omertà* ("sisters' code of silence"). They are the ones who defend the men from punitive raids, hide those who are on the run, maintain ties with those in prison, and, above all, hand down to the next generation the clan's culture and traditions. One such tradition is the placing of a knife and a key next to a newborn, in order to see which the baby touches first. If the knife, it is a sign of future service to the clan; if the key, it predicts a life as the enemy: the jailer who locks prison cells.

Hope and despair alternate down the centuries in a land that has seen many armies pass through and has been occupied for long periods.

THE MAFIA'S VICTIMS AND METHODS OF ELIMINATION

Kidnappings, strangulation, acid, shotguns. Changing methods and weapons. Murder, Inc., and the professional hit squad. Murder as punishment and means of intimidation: the culture of vendettas and "indirect revenge." The profile of the killer and victim.

"Death Chambers" and Graveyards of the Mafia

Seen from outside, it seemed an ordinary storeroom for agricultural tools, but inside it revealed all its horror. The walls were riddled with bullets and stained with blood. In the fall of 1897, the police of Palermo raided a cottage located slightly to the north of the city, among the citrus orchards at the foot of Monte Pellegrino, on an estate known as Laganà. The policemen were well aware that such farmhouses were often the scene of gun battles with the *campieri*, or armed guards, of the Mafia, who ruled like feudal lords in the countryside. On this occasion, the police were about to discover a building that would enter the history of organized crime as one of the Sicilian gangs' first slaughterhouses.[1] It was a real "death chamber" (the term for the blind alley at the end of the labyrinth of nets used in tuna fishing in Sicily) used for the execution of the condemned. Adjacent, but well hidden from prying eyes, was what stood in for a cemetery: a natural well that gave off a sickening smell from corpses in an advanced state of decomposition. The bodies had been covered with quicklime in order to render them unrecognizable, as well as to erase all traces of the massacre and repel

The sacking of a rural house in Sicily from Le Petit Journal, December 9, 1983. The Mafia has often been in conflict with brigands because it has always needed to exercise complete control over its territories. Anyone who committed robberies in prohibited zones could even be punished by death.

wild animals. This was Mafia "justice." To those who carried it out, such justice had nothing to do with murder, but with executions ordered by a tribunal composed of men of honor.

As investigators would discover, two of the bodies found on this occasion belonged to members of the Olivuzza gang, which had been implicated in the kidnapping of Audrey Whitaker, a ten-year-old girl from one of the wealthy English land-owning families in Palermo's Conca d'Oro. Audrey was kidnapped for ransom while riding on horseback on the estate of La Favorita, west of Laganà. Her captivity lasted only a few days, as her father Joshua knew the law of the land and paid the ransom without hesitation or uttering a word, especially to the authorities.

Vincenzo Lo Porto and Giuseppe Caruso, of the Olivuzza gang, had been condemned to death for their part in the kidnapping because, dissatisfied with what they were paid for taking part in Audrey's abduction, they had decided to operate on their own and to punish the bosses for the "wrong" they believed they had suffered. They stole valuable objects from the villa of one of the most prominent families in the city, the Florios, who were already paying the Olivuzza gang for protection. This theft, committed in a "protected zone" was believed by Lo Porto and Caruso to be fair compensation for their meager share of the ransom, but it was also meant as an insult to the bosses for their arrogance. The intention was to make the bosses lose face, and thereby demonstrate their inability to control their own territory. But the Mafia has always known how to wait for revenge—which is, as the

saying goes, a dish best served cold. The boss of the Olivuzza gang decided on the punishment, along with the neighboring gangs, in order to maintain the delicate territorial equilibrium among them. The thieves were persuaded to return the stolen goods in exchange for due recompense for Audrey's kidnapping. Later on, Lo Porto and Caruso were enticed to Laganà on the pretext of a new theft. They were met instead by an execution squad and the darkness of a well that went deep into the earth.

Similar Mafia cemeteries are still found in the Sicilian countryside by the police. One such was discovered at Villagrazia di Carini, about six miles outside Palermo. A few years ago, based on information received from *pentiti*, on land adjoining the highway to Mazara del Vallo, investigators discovered the remains of "soldiers" who had been put to death for disobedience, or for being in the service of rival gangs.

Whatever the historical period or the methods employed—whether executions carried out in "death chambers" deep in the countryside, murders committed in public places in broad daylight, or the mysterious disappearance of enemies and rivals—the Mafia has had two principal aims: to emphasize its absolute supremacy, and to send an unmistakable message to anyone who needs to hear it. It is for the second reason that Mafia murders are characterized by a specific system of symbols, and carried out with rituals and methods that vary depending on the particular message intended.

Murder, Inc.

"Between the law and the Mafia, it isn't the law that strikes the greater fear." This Sicilian proverb speaks volumes about the techniques refined by the gangs in order to eliminate adversaries and traitors. Illustrated newspapers from the late nineteenth century depict carabinieri and police investigators examining the victims of such bloody settlements of accounts. As time went on, these methods were perfected specifically to hinder the work of investigators, thus protecting both executioners and those who ordered the killings. In New York in the 1930s there was even a group specializing in the methodical elimination of persons considered to be "inconvenient" by the Sicilian-American families. Murder, Inc.,[*2] as it was dubbed by the *New York World-Telegram*, consisted of ten or so men from Brooklyn skilled in the use of weapons on orders from organized crime. The killers had the advantage of operating in places where they were not well known and from which they could rapidly flee. In case of arrest, they were helped by knowing nothing about the reason for the hit or who had ordered it. Their savagery was legendary. Stories abound of how one member, impatient at the service in a restaurant, stuck a fork in the unfortunate waiter's eye. Another used the chickens in his yard as target practice. And yet, they clearly operated by a code of conduct: one member refused to carry out a job on religious holidays. In every case, the assassins knew how to adjust their modus operandi to the situation at hand, using grotesquely symbolic gestures to reflect the crime. Police informants would be found with a canary

Top: Dangers of the profession. A battle between the carabinieri and members of the Camorra on the outskirts of Naples sometime around 1908.

Bottom: Kidnapping for ransom. In this case, the victim is a landowner abducted and questioned by Sicilian mafiosi. Blackmail and intimidation were used as a way to force property owners to sell their land to the gangs at low prices.

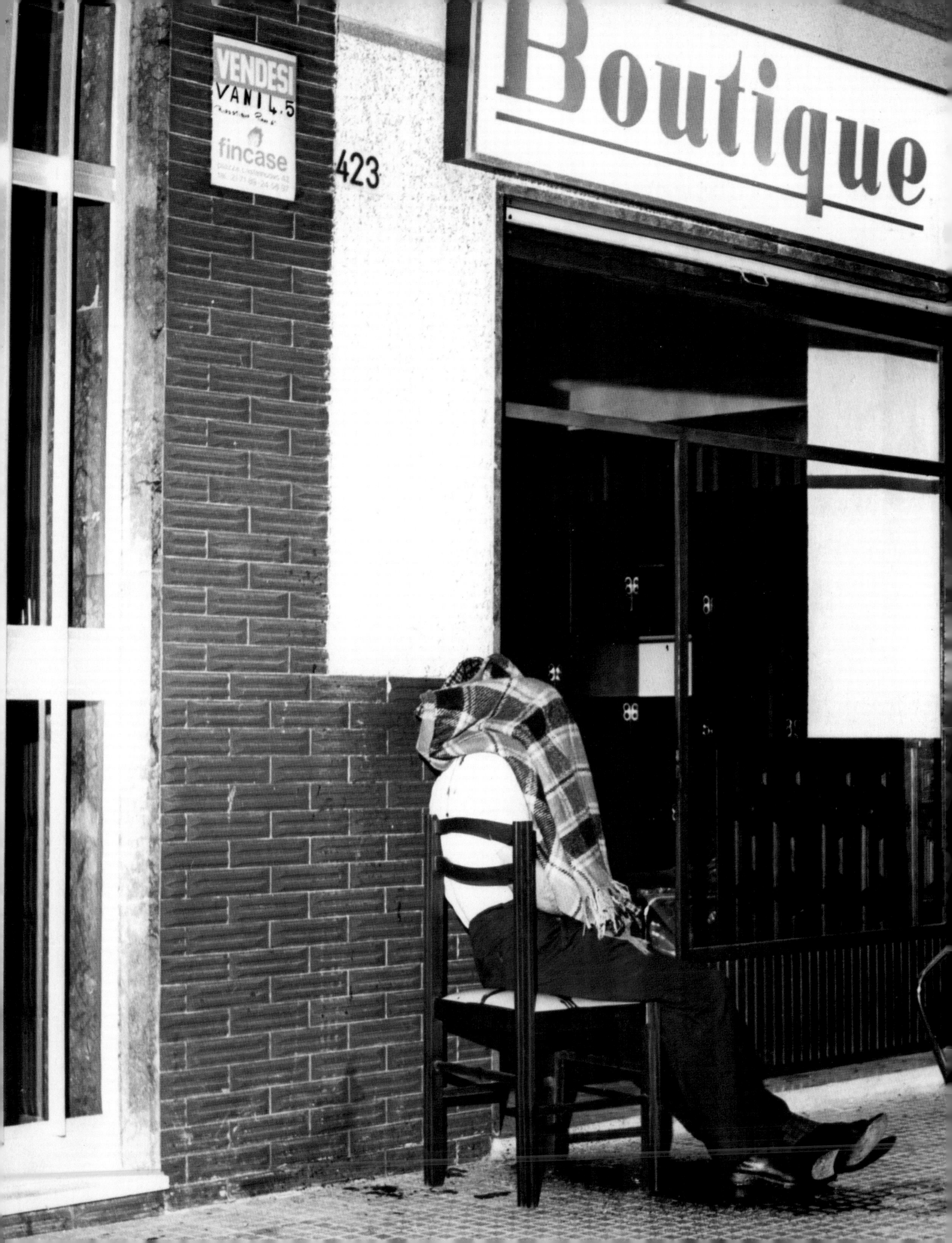
Boutique
VENDESI
VANI 4.5
fincase
423

The certainty
of punishment.
A previous offender
killed by Mafia
assassins in Palermo
in 1975 while waiting
in front of a furniture
store.

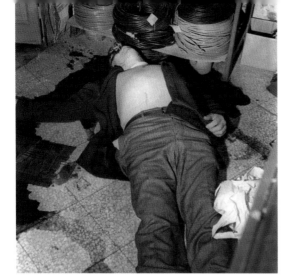

Top: A Mafia execution in the Brancaccio neighborhood of Palermo. This part of Palermo was under the ironclad control of the Mafia families who divided up the city and administered justice without appeal.

Bottom: Murders in broad daylight. Killings were often committed by unmasked criminals in front of a large crowd in an attempt to assert control over a specific territory.

or a rat stuffed in their mouths; a willingness to testify in a murder case would be punished by stabbing or pulling out the witness's eyes. Sexual harassment of a boss's wife was punishable by death and castration. In an attempt to discredit the evidence against it before its ultimate defeat, Murder, Inc. contrived a strategy reminiscent of *Hamlet*, in which the king is killed by poison poured in his ear. The victim was to be killed by an ice pick stuck deep inside the brain through the auditory canal, to lead the coroner to conclude that death was from a hemorrhage. It was a crude but effective strategy that seems to have been used even by a boss as high up as Lucky Luciano.[3]

But perhaps the most effective method was simply to make the victim disappear. Without a body there was no proof of a crime, but also no grave and no opportunity for the families to mourn. Not only did it help the perpetrator to escape detection, it sent out a clear warning to rivals who might want to behave in the same way. Finally, it extended the punishment to the victim's family in denying them a funeral, as well as the death certificate required for life insurance policies. In Sicily, this method of disappearance came to be called the *lupara bianca*—the "white shotgun"—in contrast to the *lupara rossa* (red shotgun) i.e., killings carried out with rifles.

Facing page: A lupara loaded with large-caliber shot is the classic weapon used by the Mafia. The submachine gun came into use after World War II.

The Songs of the Machine Gun and the Shotgun

The staccato rhythm of a machine gun accompanied a Mafia crime for the first time in Sicily on August 27, 1946, having arrived three years earlier with the Allied landings. Two brothers, victims of a vendetta, surprised while playing cards in front of their house in the neighborhood of Ciaculli in Palermo, fell under a burst of fire, that killed one of them.[4] The deed signaled an escalation in the use of weapons more modern and effective than the sawn-off shotgun traditionally used by the gangs. From that moment on, the machine gun would predominate in Mafia killings: a weapon of war for a war that was unending. In recent times weapons have escalated further still, to include the Kalashnikov assault rifle, the Skorpion submachine gun, the French Mauser, and the Uzi light machine gun. These instruments of death were extraordinarily effective, creating terror by the destruction they caused. They also guaranteed the success of military operations, such as when they were used to shatter the glass of an armored car carrying a passenger under armed escort. Such weapons were routinely hidden in underground bunkers belonging to the gangs and which, in Naples at least, were occasionally also commandeered by Camorra bosses to stash sun lamps to top up their suntans.

Underground bunkers are used to hide both weapons manufactured all over the world, and men.

"Indirect Revenge" and Acid Baths

In Sicily the term "indirect revenge*" is used for murders committed to strike back at a *pentito** by killing a relative who had no involvement in the decision to side with the authorities. No victim was treated savagely more than Giuseppe Di Matteo, who was kidnapped at the age of thirteen, held for two years and three months and passed around to almost one hundred different people before being strangled and dissolved in a vat of nitric acid.[5] Giovanni Brusca was the boss of the village of San Giuseppe Jato, and had been responsible for the detonation of the car bomb that killed Giovanni Falcone, his wife, and his escort on May 23, 1992. When an accomplice, Mario Santo Di Matteo, was arrested the following month, his confessions threatened to bring down the whole gang. In order to force a retraction, Brusca ordered the abduction of Di Matteo's son, Giuseppe, while he was riding on November 23, 1993,[6] at Villabate, a property belonging to other men of honor. "While Giuseppe was hidden in the province of Agrigento," Brusca confessed after his arrest and decision to cooperate with the authorities, "I opened the first channels of communication with the family."[7] At regular intervals the family received photos of Guiseppe with a copy of the daily newspaper, along with messages dictated to him, such as "Put a cork in it," and sent to his father in prison. Brusca stated in his confession, "I asked the boy to write small notes to get the grandfather to speak with the father and make him retract."[8] The grandfather did everything he could to save his grandson, but to no avail. Brusca heard news that he had been sentenced to life in prison while he was living as a fugitive. As punishment for his father Mario's cooperation with the authorities, Brusca gave the order to kill Giuseppe.

That same punishment continued to be meted out: in 2000 a Mafia foot soldier, suspected of murdering the son of one of the Palermo bosses, met the same fate. He was kidnapped while in his car with his seven-year-old daughter, taken to the countryside and suffocated, and his body dissolved in acid. His fate was revealed to the Palermo police by his daughter's drawings.

"Indirect revenge." Giuseppe Di Matteo was held prisoner for two years before being strangled and dissolved in acid because his father was a Mafia pentito.

The savagery of the Mafia knows no bounds, especially when it comes to punishing a traitor. These include auto-strangulation, in which the victim is tied with a rope around the ankles and hands, while the other end of the rope is tied around the neck. When the position can no longer be maintained and the muscles that keep the legs bent back toward the head start to relax, the rope around the neck tightens, suffocating the victim. But the method of execution feared the most is to be stabbed and thrown to a herd of ravenous pigs in a cement enclosure. The scent of fresh blood sends the starved animals into a frenzy and they will eat the condemned man alive.

Import-Export Executions

Guns of all description are used not only in the endless struggle for Mafia territory, but also in order to eliminate judges harmful to the interests

of the organization. Wielding these weapons are often killers coming from overseas, capable of striking without pity and then vanishing into thin air. These "import-export" assassins working for the Mafia are more difficult to capture once they've returned to the United States among the waves of legitimate immigrants from Sicily. Sicilians were behind the elimination in a shoot-out of Carmine "Lilo" Galante, on July 12, 1979, while he dined at a restaurant in Brooklyn.[9] His possible ascent to the upper reaches of the Bonanno family, one of the five crime families that shared in the Big Apple's illegal trafficking, had become a problem for the Sicilian mafia, who wanted to open up a new channel for the drug trade in the United States. Another victim of "import-export" killing was recent Sicilian immigrant Pietro Inzerillo, killed on January 15, 1982, in Mount Laurel, New Jersey, by Corleonesi-contracted killers sent to make a clean sweep during the second Mafia war over control of the heroin trade that had broken out in Palermo.[10] His body, riddled with bullets, was found with five dollars stuffed in the mouth and two on the genitals, a sign that the victim had stolen money from the organization.[11]

In Sicily, the Stidda (Sicilian dialect for "star") of Agrigento, a criminal organization in conflict with the Mafia, employed German killers to do their dirty work. Their job was to eliminate Judge Rosario Livatino, known as the Boy Judge, and who had, at age thirty-seven, successfully captured Mafia fortunes through strict application of the law regarding the preventative seizure of property. On September 21, 1990, he drove without an escort the SS 640 Road on the way to Caltanissetta. Bullets shattered the rear window of the car while it was crossing a viaduct, providing no means of escape. Despite his attempt to flee down a hillside he was apprehended and shot—his last words "Why? What have I done to you?" His killers returned to Germany but were later caught and sentenced to life in prison.

Victims Caught in the Crossfire

The Mafia has often killed the wrong person, and not just in Sicily. It happened, for example, during the years of the feuds between the emerging clans in Palermo, in August 1956, when a twelve-year-old girl named Giuseppina Savoca was caught in a drive-by shooting on the via Messina Marine.[12] It also happened on the evening of April 22, 1999, when Stefano Pompeo, an eleven-year-old accompanying his father in a jeep belonging to a Mafia boss, was shot in a case of mistaken identity by a rival gang. But innocent deaths are not just caused by bullets. Every year, on the road from Pizzolungo to Trapani, there is a memorial for the massacre that took place on April 2, 1985, when Barbara Asta and her six-year-old twin sons

Salvatore and Giuseppe received the full force of a bomb intended for Judge Carlo Palermo. The armor-plated Alfa Romeo carrying the judge passed the small passenger car driven by Barbara at the exact spot where the explosive device had been placed. The killers pressed the button on the detonator just the same. The Asta family's car shielded the judge's, which saved his life, while the scattered remains of the Asta family were found dozens of yards away.[13] Like the Asta family, many of the innocent victims

had no connection whatsoever with the Mafia. Ida Castellucci was five months pregnant when she was killed on August 5, 1989, in the town of Villagrazia di Carini while in a car with her policeman husband, Antonio Agostino. Despite the twenty-year fight for justice by Antonio's father, Vicenzo, the Italian judiciary has not been able to solve the case.

Rest in Peace Radio Aut

Some are born to oppose the Mafia, such as the priest, Don Giuseppe Puglisi, who was assassinated by the Mafia on September 15, 1993, because he tried to rescue teenagers who had been recruited by it. But others born within the Mafia itself may turn against the organization. Such was the case of Peppino Impastato, whose father Luigi, for many years a gang member in the town of Cinisi, had been interned during the Fascist era because of his illegal activities. Peppino did not want to follow in his father's footsteps. He joined the militant Proletarian Democracy Party, a small Marxist group, and fought for a more just society. In 1977 he founded Radio Aut, a self-financed, independent broadcasting station. Imitating the Mafia bosses' voices on air, he would denounce their activities, including the international drug trade, which operated even at Palermo's Punta Raisi Airport. A favorite target of Peppino's transmissions was Gaetano Badalamenti, the leader of the "Pizza Connection" and the Mafia's *Capo dei Capi*. Peppino openly ridiculed him on his wildly popular radio program. But his outspokenness cost him his life, when, on May 8, 1978, mafiosi tied his lifeless body to some railroad tracks along with a charge

Left: Domenico Agostino refused to shave his beard until the authorities revealed the truth about the deaths of his son Agostino and his daughter-in-law Ida Castellucci.

Facing page: Some actively fought to halt the power of the gangs, even those born with Mafia connections. Don Giuseppe Puglisi (left) fought to prevent young men from being recruited by the gangs. Peppino Impastato (right), the son of a gang member, founded a radio station in order to tell the world the truth about Don Tano Badalamenti.

of explosives, in order to make it seem the work of terrorists and divert suspicion from the gangs.[14] However, Peppino's mother Felicia would break the wall of silence usually imposed on Mafia women and helped to reopen the investigations into his death. In 2002 Gaetano Badalamenti was sentenced to life in prison for ordering Peppino's murder.

Other opponents of the Mafia have met similar fates, and the lists of their victims fill hundreds of books and judicial records. Among them are journalists such as Mauro de Mauro, who disappeared in 1970, and his colleague Giovanni Spampinato, killed two years later, both fearless investigative journalists for Palermo daily newspaper *L'Ora*. Another on the list would

be Giuseppe Fava, the journalist and playwright killed by the Mafia in 1984. The list also includes brave entrepreneurs such as Libero Grassi, murdered in broad daylight in the center of town in 1991 for having publicly refused to pay the *pizzo**, or extortion tax, imposed by the gangs on anyone who wanted to work in areas under their control. In Puglia, the uncontested domain of another Mafia-type organization, the Sacra Corona Unita, gang members in 1991 abducted twenty-seven-year-old Paola Rizzello along with her two-year-old daughter, Angelica Pirtoli. The two were strangled and killed on the orders of a local boss, Paola's lover, who was himself pushed to commit the double murder by his wife, who wanted to eliminate a rival after discovering her husband's infidelity.

These victims leave a long and indelible trail of blood. They are remembered today on gravestones, in memorial gardens, or on commemorative plaques. In Rome a luxurious villa confiscated from a Mafia boss has now been turned into a music venue. It bears a plaque paying tribute to his six hundred victims.

Left: Lupara bianca (literally "white shotgun," meaning a murder without a gun and where the body is never found). Shortly before his disappearance, Mauro de Mauro, the author of several investigations into drug trafficking, was working on the screenplay for a film about the death of Enrico Mattei, the president of the Italian oil and gas corporation ENI. According to officials, Mattei died in an airplane accident, but according to some pentiti he was assassinated by the Mafia.

Facing page: Courageous businessman. Libero Grassi paid with his life for his rebellion against the law of the pizzo.

THE MASSACRE OF DUISBURG: THE 'NDRANGHETA ARRIVES IN GERMANY

On August 15, 2007, Duisburg, a city in the mining area of the Ruhr Basin in Germany, saw the massacre of six young Italian men at a pizza parlor. It was the culmination of sixteen long years of feuds and vendettas that had started in San Luca, Calabria, in 1991, when what began as a joke at the local carnival escalated into a quarrel and violence that would see two local men dead. The men belonged to a 'Ndrangheta family; the perpetrators were from a rival family. Over the course of the feud there were fatalities on both sides, despite a truce called in 2000. By 2007 the retaliations had intensified and it is thought that the six assassinated in Germany had fled to escape the violence. They were mistaken.

The massacre in Duisburg was the largest in 'Ndrangheta history; the bodies were returned to San Luca in an atmosphere of almost unbearable tension, with the local area heavily policed to prevent more violence.

The episode revealed in a most tragic way the extent of the 'Ndrangheta's influence beyond Italy, suggesting an organization more powerful and more savage than the Sicilian Mafia.

L'Unità reports the Duisburg massacre. Horror, death and fear, San Luca is armed: according to the left-wing Italian daily, arms and drug trafficking lie behind the feud.

CHRONOLOGY OF A MASSACRE FORETOLD

February 10, 1991: In the village of San Luca, a brawl between two rival families belonging to the Nirta-Strangio and Pelle-Vottari clans turns into tragedy. It starts in a bar with an egg thrown as a joke in celebration of Carnival. Two members of the Nirta-Strangio family are killed.

May 1, 1993: It is Labor Day but the pistols in San Luca are not idle. Four people are shot dead, two from each warring clan.

July 31, 2006: An ally of the Vottari clan is wounded and suffers permanent damage to his spinal column.

Christmas 2006: The female relative of a member of the Strangio clan is murdered. The Mafia code of honor dictates that women and children must always be spared from violence and so, when this rule is broken, the hatred and desire for vengeance have no bounds.

August 15, 2007: The San Luca feud arrives in Duisburg, Germany. Late at night, in front of the Italian pizzeria "Da Bruno," six people connected to the Pelle-Vottari family are massacred. Two killers lying in wait behind some bushes fire 54 shots at their targets as they leave the restaurant, and then finish them off as they lie on the ground dying. The youngest victim is just sixteen. Inside the restaurant the investigators find a .223-caliber Remington assault rifle along with a prayer book. In the wallet of one of the victims is a half-burned image of the Archangel Michael, the kind used in the initiation rites of the 'Ndrangheta. The restaurant has now changed management, and its shop sign has been sold on the Internet for several thousand euros to a collector of objects related to organized crime. In San Luca, it seems that peace has returned because, as someone said to a reporter, "revenge costs too much money."

THE **WAR** ON THE **MAFIA**: JUDGES AND **POLICEMEN** **ALONE** AGAINST THE **OCTOPUS**

Lone policemen and government officials who made a stand against the Mafia. The murder of detective Joe Petrosino in the early 1900s. Fascism and the Mafia: Prefect Mori's efforts to end the banditry in Sicily. The years of silence and political cover-ups. The growth in organized crime, the reaction of the Italian state, and the Mafia's revenge. The murder of Paolo Borsellino and Giovanni Falcone in the late 1980s.

Army of fugitives. Among old identification photos used by the police in the search for fugitives is one of Totò Riina (pictured second from left, third row from the top).

Identification Photos of Bandits and Mafiosi

The period photos, yellowed with age, are posed as if for a portrait. Sometimes the subject is already dead: killed in gun battles with the authorities or shot at point-blank range as conspirators against the new Kingdom of Italy. Images of bandits and mafiosi held in archives and private collections tell the history of crime photography that, since 1860 in Sicily, was used as an investigative tool in the hunt for those on the run, and for keeping files on those in prison.[1] From the start, the army that controlled the territory used such images as tools of propaganda. Bandits were seen as an unacceptable social evil for the future unified Italian state. Explicit photographs of their corpses, laid out in grotesque poses and even decapitated, as if they were trophies, were used as part of this campaign and kept alive a tradition that went back to the Middle Ages, when the head of an executed person would be displayed in a prominent public place as a deterrent against crime. In the second half of the nineteenth century the photograph was able to serve a similar purpose. In 1859, André Adolphe Eugène Disdéri, an enterprising French photographer, took a photographic portrait of Napoleon III, the Empress Eugénie, and their young heir, which was truly revolutionary for an aristocratic family accustomed to portrait painting. That moment sparked a craze for *cartes de visite*, small photographs approximately $2^{1/2} \times 3^{1/2}$ inches in size, which became popular among all social classes and were produced in the millions. This led, simultaneously and almost accidentally, to the identification photo, when portraits from private albums began to appear in files maintained by the authorities as a means of identifying suspects. More refined methods were already in use in England, where, in 1870, a law was instated requiring the systematic photographing of all those held in custody, which created a police archive. In 1871 the French police, alarmed by the social turmoil fostered by the Paris Commune, hired photographers to document the resulting acts of vandalism, as a way of tracking those who were responsible. It led to the setting up of a genuine photography studio for use by the authorities. The images were used by Prefect Alphonse Bertillon in 1879 when he developed "identification anthropometry," based on a complex system of measurements for the identification of criminals.[2]

Joe Petrosino Defies the Mafia

On the evening of March 12, 1909, Giuseppe Michele Pasquale Petrosino, known as Joe Petrosino, was struck by three shots from a pistol in Piazza Marina in Palermo. His body fell on the pavement of the Garibaldi gardens near a streetcar stop. Some distance away lay the derby hat he was accustomed to wearing. There were no photos or police files in the pockets of his overcoat, but there was a precious notebook, filled with lists of Sicilians who had previously been convicted of crimes, and, at the end, the name of the person who had arranged his murder, with, perhaps, the names of his assassins, professional killers who had fired at close range.

So ended the life of the only police official of the State of New York ever killed while on an overseas mission in the long war against the Mafia in Sicily.[3] Joe Petrosino was born in the village of Padula in the Campania region of southern Italy on

Detective story. The exploits of the famous Italian-American policeman who fought the Black Hand in New York in the early twentieth century have inspired generations of writers and illustrators, as seen in this Italian comic book of the time.

Fascicolo N. 1   RACCONTO COMPLETO   Prezzo L. 25

PETROSINO

IL GRANDE POLIZIOTTO ITALO-AMERICANO

Da spazzino a Capo di Polizia

Petrosino gridò; — Mani in alto! Chi non si arrende sarà ucciso. — Col pugnale alla mano tentarono reagire, ma si calmarono presto sotto la minaccia infallibile delle rivoltelle del poliziotto.

August 30, 1860, and later emigrated to the United States with his parents. He was professionally tenacious, an expert in disguises and in undercover operations, even infiltrating New York construction sites dressed as a workman in order to gather information. Petrosino knew every deed and misdeed committed in the Italian neighborhoods of New York. He specialized in the fight against extortion of small businesses by the Black Hand, active in New York and other American cities at the turn of the twentieth century. But it was his involvement in the investigation of the so-called "barrel murder" that ultimately sent Petrosino to his death. The investigation was launched on April 14, 1903, following the discovery in an abandoned container of a man who had been stabbed to death, his genitals stuffed in his mouth, a sign of a Mafia-related crime. Petrosino traced the crime to a group of Sicilians being investigated in Italy for, among other things, the murder of Emanuele Notarbartolo, the director of the Bank of Sicily. One of the members of the group was Don Vito Cascio Ferro, born in Sambuca Zabut, near Agrigento, and at the time living in Bisaquino, near Palermo. "A dangerous criminal," according to the notebook found on Petrosino the night he was murdered in Palermo.

Petrosino had been devoted to investigating Mafia activity since 1905, when, alarmed by the increase of attacks by the Black Hand, the local New York City government had set up a small specialized police squad called the Italian Branch dedicated to investigating crimes of extortion. Three years later, thanks to the initiative of Chief of Police Theodore A. Bingham and to funds provided by wealthy members of the Italian community, a true covert

operation was established, with greater freedom of action than the regular authorities in the search for evidence against the Mafia gangs. At the same time, however, the preventive measures put into effect in Sicily by the Italian government left much to be desired. Members of the Mafia continued to pour into the United States thanks to the channels offered by illegal immigration. The only way to stop the flow of traffic and to expose the import and export of Mafia bosses between Old World and New was to create, in Sicily, a secret information network to work closely with the American police and to obtain information from sources on the island, including court archives. In early 1909, Joe Petrosino planned to travel to Italy on a secret mission, with the task of establishing just such a network and of researching the police records of suspicious individuals. But on February 20 of that year, the *New York Herald* newspaper unexpectedly published news of his trip to Sicily. Nonetheless, the detective continued with his trip and arrived in Palermo on February 28, lodging at the Hotel de France in Piazza Marina under an assumed name.

But Petrosino had underestimated the power of the enemy. After his murder, investigators found a regulation Smith & Wesson .38-caliber pistol still packed in his suitcase. Petrosino was not afraid of surprises, but clearly was not expecting the greeting he received that evening in the Piazza Marina where he had gone to meet someone claiming to provide information. Four bullets rent the air and three hit their target, two in the back of the neck and one in the face. Back in New York, he was given a hero's funeral. His wife, his three-month-old daughter, and other family members were among the more than

On the hunt for the Mafia. Joe Petrosino left New York for Italy in an attempt to identify the connections between the American Cosa Nostra and the Sicilian Mafia.

Mission impossible. Petrosino, assassinated in Palermo, with an honor guard of police in New York. Over 200,000 mourners lined the streets as the funeral cortège wended its way through the city and proceeded along Fifth Avenue. The city of Manhattan declared the day of the funeral a day of mourning.

two hundred thousand people who accompanied his coffin as it was followed by carriages, officials, honor guards, and men on horseback through the most important streets of the city. When it reached Fifth Avenue the cortège broke up and the hearse continued on its journey to Calvary cemetery.

Mussolini Sends the Iron Prefect to Sicily

Don Vito Cascio Ferro was born in 1862. He liked English tailoring and wore elegant clothes purchased in Palermo's exclusive Bustarino boutique on Via Maqueda. He frequented the theater and high-society salons. But, like many men from the countryside, the boss of Bisaquino, an agricultural town in the southernmost part of the province of Palermo, was almost illiterate. He claimed to be a peasant, but became rich thanks to livestock theft. At the end of the nineteenth century he sided with the tenant farmers and Socialists, not for idealistic reasons but for profit. The most astute bosses understood that by helping the sharecroppers in their struggle against the large landowners for better economic conditions, they could also obtain advantages for themselves. Many mafiosi became *gabellotti*, or tax collectors, renting the land on a kind of tax lease, and if the level of social tension became too great, then the landowner would sooner or later feel pushed to get rid of the land, selling it to the boss for a ridiculously low price. The boss would keep the most profitable part for himself and transfer another part to the local agricultural bank in order to finance "friendly" business people. Or he might use it as a way to give new employment to the workers' cooperatives, thus reinforcing his

influence at the local level. Don Vito was the prime suspect in the murder of detective Joe Petrosino, but was acquitted thanks to powerful supporters and a watertight alibi.

In 1913, the right to vote in elections in Italy was extended to the entire adult male population, but this also served to reinforce the power of the gangs, whose relationship with the upper classes became ever more entwined. By the end of World War I, Italy underwent a series of transformations that would lead just a few years later to the arrival of Fascism, which would abrogate all democratic freedoms in order to impose a new political and social order.

In 1921 the city of Palermo experienced an intense period of economic crisis.[4] The peasants who had served in the army returned from the front demanding a more equitable say in the management of land. The legally controlled rents on the estates only served to increase the insatiable appetites of the bosses, who continued to buy up new land, resorting to sabotage by cutting down trees and vines if necessary.[5] The arrogance of respectable society was now greater than its level of vigilance against the underworld, and in Benito Mussolini, the Fascist leader who came to power on October 22, 1922, the landed aristocracy of Sicily saw a way out of their own inexorable decline. Fascism saw in the losing cause of those impoverished nobles the perfect opportunity to bring order and security back to Sicily, giving it the stability, under the guise of reform, that earlier liberal governments had been unable to achieve. This heralded a sea change, too, in the relationship between the Mafia and the government, as the Mafia attempted to curry favor

Cesare Mori, the "Iron Prefect" here in a portrait dressed for the countryside, was given special powers by Mussolini in the endless war between the Italian state and the Sicilian gangs.

S. E. Cesare Mori, in tenuta.... di campagna.

with the Fascist dictator and his militia (the Camicie Nere, or Black Shirts). To this end, many took part in the overthrow of Socialist administrations that were hostile to the dictatorship, and in the breaking up of the cooperatives and rural associations that until then had been skillfully exploited by them against the property owners and landed estates.

But the Fascists, like all dictatorships, did not want intermediaries. To exercise power they needed direct contact with the masses.[6] Between 1924 and 1925, the regime accomplished the abolition of civil liberties and, with the definitive modification of the election laws in 1928, it took from the Mafia its most effective way of putting pressure on politicians: control of local votes. The town councils were dissolved and administration of the cities passed directly under the control of the *podestà*, an official who answered only to Mussolini. But the Fascist regime weakened Mafia power directly, too, by launching a violent program of repression against the criminal organizations. It was directed by Cesare

Mori (1871–1942) who, after Mussolini's visit to Sicily, was named prefect of Palermo on October 23, 1925. Mori had unlimited power and soon became known as the Iron Prefect for his unwavering campaign against the Mafia. In 1926 alone, eleven thousand people were arrested, among them Don Vito Cascio Ferro (who would later be sentenced to life in prison for instigating three murders in 1930). By the end of that year, the number of murders had dropped to 77 compared to 268 the year before. But the means of arrest and of extracting confession were severe: those on the run were made to give themselves up by the threat of deportation of their families, the summary slaughter of their livestock, and the bulk sale of their possessions. Confessions were obtained by methods that included electric shock.[7] Judges were able to sentence hundreds of suspects in a single proceeding, because in order to reach a guilty verdict it was necessary only to demonstrate that the accused belonged to a criminal association and not that he had committed any specific crime. To further destroy their influence, bosses and associates were interned in places far from their homes and businesses. And if by chance the judges were to acquit the accused, the Iron Prefect would intervene with measures that could be enforced on anyone merely suspected of gang involvement.

As Mori would write in his memoirs, through these measures, the landowners were "freed from the chains"[8] that had enslaved them in their homeland. Mussolini's "remedy" for dealing with the Mafia had unprecedented results, but, according to some historians, it remained incomplete because it was directed mostly at the unskilled workers on the lower rungs of the Mafia and spared the higher-ups who had infiltrated and were in collusion with the government. In casting its net so wide it also caught many innocent people who were unjustly punished for the crimes of the underworld. Others are of the opinion that Fascism destroyed the Sicilian Mafia, but only temporarily, and that it would revive and become stronger than ever due to the support provided by the Anglo-American landings of 1943. What remains without doubt, however, is that it had been hit by the regime in a brutal way. Most likely, the groups that were able to endure were those that had been established the longest and had the deepest roots in the territory.[9]

In 1929 Mori retired from his position as prefect and became a senator in the national parliament. Don Vito Cascio Ferro is believed to have died in prison of natural causes in 1945, although rumors persist that he had died some years earlier, abandoned by guards who evacuated all the other inmates due to the threat of Allied bombardment. While in prison he had let it be understood that he had been Joe Petrosino's killer more than thirty years earlier in Palermo. It is said that on a wall in his prison cell he had scratched the phrase: *Vicaria, malatia e nicissitati, si vidi lu' cori de l'amicu,* which is Sicilian dialect for "Prison, illness, and poverty reveal the heart of the old friend." Those "friends," pushed by Fascist repression, had in the meanwhile emigrated to the United States and, at the end of wartime hostilities, would contribute to the revival of the Mafia on an international scale.

No Funeral for the Mafia. Italian Investigators Alone Against the Octopus

"A funeral for the Mafia? But the Mafia doesn't exist," politicians at the highest levels of central government in Rome often said.[10] In the 1950s Italy was being reconstructed: the country had suffered greatly during the war and even Palermo was rebuilding. Real estate speculation and the rapidly expanding contracts sector became, along with drug trafficking, the main course of action for the insatiable appetites of the bosses. The authorities once again turned a blind eye, allowing Mafia business to run rampant. In 1962 what became known as the first Mafia war for control of the drug trade broke out, led by Luciano Leggio and Totò Riina from Corleone and featuring a mix of alliances and betrayals marked by a long chain of murders and bomb attacks intended to crush adversaries. On June 30, 1963, however, a high-powered car bomb meant to kill Salvatore Greco in the clan's stronghold in the Palermo suburbs missed its target and killed seven carabinieri. A punctured tire had forced the Mafia to abandon the car, which was later approached by the soldiers as the device detonated.[11] As public alarm escalated, the government had to be seen to be acting and new laws were passed to increase police power in the fight against the Mafia, such as internment out of the local region. Later the investigations into the assassinations of magistrates Pietro Scaglione in 1971 and Cesare Terranova in 1979 would pave the way for a series of high-profile Mafia trials.

Some of the most powerful bosses were forced to go into hiding, but the machine gun attacks and bombings did not stop. Hit men disguised as

Top: The entrance to the road in the Palermo suburb of Villa Sirena di Ciaculli. The car packed with explosives meant for Salvatore Greco passed through here.

Bottom: The hole created by the explosion, which accidentally killed seven carabinieri.

An immense crowd of soldiers and civilians throngs Corso Vittorio Emanuele in Palermo to take part in the funeral of the victims of the massacre of Ciaculli. But the awakening was only temporary. As often happens in Sicily, omertà, the Mafia's law of silence, proved stronger than the people's anger.

"Excellent cadavers*". Officials line up behind the coffins of the carabinieri who were torn to pieces by the car bomb manufactured by the Mafia.

policemen took part in the massacre of Viale Lazio, on December 10, 1969, in the basement of one of the palaces in the gardens of the Conca d'Oro outside Palermo. And on the night of October 28, 1970, four killers disguised as patients shot and killed a former Mafia *campiere* (armed guard) in the hospital where he was recovering from a knife attack. The investigations intensified and many bosses ended up in court, even if the trials, which took place in regions of southern Italy other than Sicily in order to avoid undue influencing of the judges, came to nothing. In 1969 Luciano Leggio, along with sixty-three others, was acquitted due to insufficient evidence.[12]

The gangs profited from the state's impotence and expanded their territory to other parts of Italy and overseas. Nonetheless, investigators continued to exert pressure on the gangs and as a consequence, murders committed to intimidate those working for the authorities became more frequent. Those who fell around the time of the second Mafia war included carabinieri colonel Giuseppe Russo in 1977; carabinieri captain Emanuele Basile, out walking with his four-year-old daughter in 1980; and judge Gaetano Costa, also in 1980. In 1983 it was the turn of Rocco Chinnici, the judge who started the first anti-Mafia pool to share information among prosecutors in Palermo. He was killed by a car bomb placed near his home, along with two military escorts and the building's porter.

The gangs' bullets even reached the flying squad of the Palermo police, starting with its chief investigators. In 1979 they assassinated Boris Giuliano, the deputy administrator, who was investigating narcotics traffic in cooperation with the American authorities. In the summer of 1985, in quick succession, two commissioners paid with their lives for their zeal in the struggle against the Mafia and the arrest of several fugitives: Beppe Montana, shot while returning from a boat trip, and Ninni Cassarà, shot while entering his front door and in full view of his wife and daughter waiting on the balcony. The events surrounding Cassarà's death illustrate the isolation in which officials who pursued the gangs were forced to live. Cassarà had informed his wife of his arrival by telephone, but it is suspected the call was intercepted and passed on to the commando group of fifteen men armed with Kalashnikov rifles that had been posted at the windows of the house opposite.[13] Cassarà and Roberto Antiochia, the young agent from the arresting squad in Palermo, had no chance of escape and were cut down in hail of bullets.

There is no doubt that the Mafia had been able to count on the help of corrupt officials in order to carry out similar murders. Accusations of such collusion would hit high-level members of the Italian intelligence agencies. One of them was Bruno Contrada, an official who was put on trial for aiding and abetting the Mafia. Other informers who became part of the diverse world of the criminal organizations were punished and dissolved in acid, such as Emanuele Piazza, another traitor in the intelligence services, who disappeared in March 1990. However, in recent years, thanks to the use of specialized anti-crime units and ever more effective methods of espionage—such as micro-circuit cameras or electronic bugs—the authorities have had more success in their fight against the gangs. The era of judges and investigators abandoned by their own institutions to face alone an "octopus" with "the enormous power of a modern state"[14] had come to an end.

Judges Falcone and Borsellino: Whose Side Is the State On?

Giovanni Falcone was able to delineate the structure of the Sicilian Mafia, thanks in part to the statements of Tommaso Buscetta. This opened the way for the maxi-trials of 1986.

Giovanni Falcone and Paolo Borsellino were also abandoned by a state "deeply polluted by collusion"[15] between a certain part of the Italian political class and the Mafia. Both were victims in separate bomb attacks organized by the gangs in the terrible summer of 1992. They were part of the anti-Mafia pool led by Antonino Caponnetto of the Palermo prosecutor's office, which shared information about Mafia activities among prosecutors in an attempt to bring about more convictions. The pool succeeded in bringing to trial some 475 defendants, in the so-called maxi-trials against the Mafia, which began on February 10, 1986, in the purpose-built bunker hall near the Ucciardone prison in Palermo. The pool made use of Falcone's and Borsellino's ability to gain the trust

of those *pentiti* ready to reveal the internal workings of the Mafia's Commission, the organization that served as a kind of board of directors in the approval of a series of dreadful crimes and murders. Tommaso Buscetta was among them, a *pentito* who had decided to turn his back on the Mafia once and for all. It was his and the testimony of others like him who brought the bosses to trial.

Falcone had joined the prosecutor's office in Palermo in 1982 following experience investigating financial crimes relating to the Mafia's drug trade. Falcone's investigation was international in scope and put him in contact with authorities in other countries, allowing him to trace money laundering to countries outside Italy. The days of easily traceable Mafia bank accounts were long gone. Now, to avoid the risk of discovery, the Mafia closed its heroin refineries in Sicily and began to acquire pure product from other parties, which was then bartered for other drugs such as cocaine, in order to avoid massive transfers of money.

Borsellino's experience was also crucial to the pool; he was a kind of human archive of the investigations and relationships between the Mafia groups and interests in southwestern Sicily, in particular the area around Trapani. Falcone's and Borsellino's professional lives were closely intertwined and a clear threat to the interests of the Sicilian Mafia, especially after the Court of Cassation—Italy's court of final appeal—in large part confirmed, in February 1992, the sentences handed down in the maxi-trial of six years earlier. Falcone was murdered at 5:58 p.m. on May 23, 1992, by the Mafia explosion that destroyed a stretch of highway between Palermo and the Punta Raisi airport, along with his wife and the men of his escort as their cars passed near the town of Capaci. Paolo Borsellino would be killed, along with five law enforcement agents, on July 19 of that same year, by a car bomb in Via d'Amelio in Palermo, while on his way to visit his mother.

WHEN THE MAFIA DECIDED TO MAKE A HIGHWAY JUMP

"They had told us that when Falcone would go from Punta Raisa to Palermo the speed was 80 to 85 miles per hour; it was always that."[1] Giovanni Brusca, known in local dialect as a *scannacristiani* (someone who cuts the throat of Christians), was an expert in remote-control explosions. But this time the explosion would need to be large enough to shock the world. Brusca and the men assigned to kill Judge Giovanni Falcone prepared themselves for the great attack (*l'attentatuni*, as it would be known in Sicilian dialect) with great precision. They chose a tunnel underneath a highway that Falcone and his escort had to cross over on their way from Punta Raisa airport to Palermo, at the junction for Capaci. They filled it with more than 750 pounds. of explosives packed in twelve drums that were stuffed into the opening using a skateboard. The explosion would be set off by remote control from a hill some 1,200 feet away. They tested the velocity in order to calculate the exact moment in which to set off the charge and placed a refrigerator near the roadway as a point of reference. A car was assigned to follow the judge at a distance from the moment of his arrival at the airport in order to signal his movements from place to place by means of coded messages sent by cell phone. The armored Fiat Croma driven by the judge, with his wife Francesca Morvillo, also a judge, in the car, and a driver who sat behind him, was preceded by an escort car that carried three agents, Antonio Montinari, Rocco di Cillo, and Vito Schifani. When the car reached the refrigerator it slowed to around 50 or 55 miles per hour. Brusca decided to wait a fraction of a second, even though a man with binoculars standing next to him urged him to press the button. At 5:58 p.m. on May 23, 1992, that stretch of highway became an inferno. The explosion sent asphalt 300 feet into the air. Falcone and his wife were killed, along with the agents in the escort car. Twenty other people were wounded.

1. Saverio Lodato, *Ho ucciso Giovanni Falcone, la confessione di Giovanni Brusca* (Milan: Mondadori, 1999), 94 ff.

THE LAST CIGARETTE OF THE JUDGE WHO DID NOT CARE FOR PALERMO

One of Borsellino's last inquests would have examined the connections between the Mafia, politics, and Freemasonry, charging politicians, judges, and godfathers with corruption.[1] But the Sicilian magistrate, a candidate to be the anti-Mafia "Super Procuratore," who famously did not care for Palermo but who had learned to love it, did not have time to bring the inquest to completion. On May 19, 1992, a few weeks after the massacre of Giovanni Falcone, Borsellino was likewise murdered, together with his escort, by a car bomb. It happened in the early afternoon, the killer lying in wait with a remote control device in a palazzo that was under construction. He looked in the direction of Via d'Amelio at a Fiat 126 that was loaded with more than 100 pounds. of high-powered plastic explosives. Borsellino's mother lived at no. 21 on that street and he often went to visit her. The cars in Borsellino's escort slipped through the half-empty streets of

the city, climbed to the intersection of Via Belgio, skirted the Favorita stadium, and crossed the bridge at Via dell'Autonomia Siciliana. They had arrived at their destination. Borsellino smoked his umpteenth cigarette. The first car, driven by Antonio Vullo, parked on a diagonal, in case of a needed getaway, as taught by the instruction manual for agents attached to the escort squad. Other members of the group were Emanuela Loi, age twenty-five, Walter Cusina, Claudio Traina, Vincenzo Li Muli, and Agostino Catalano. Borsellino got out of his car and approached the front door. The man with the remote control pressed the trigger and Via d'Amelio became the scene of a bloodbath. Borsellino and the police officers died instantly. One hundred thirteen families lost their homes. Among the bodies on the ground was that of Emanuela, the first female police officer killed in a Mafia ambush.

"I am optimistic because young Sicilians today have an attitude which is different from the shameful indifference that I maintained until I was in my forties." Paolo Borsellino wrote these words four days before his death, in response to a letter from a professor in Padua who asked him to define the Mafia.

---

1. Umberto Lucentini, *Paolo Borsellino, il valore di una vita* (Milan: San Paolo Edizioni, 2006), 300.

THE GREAT *PENTITI:*
FROM TOMMASO BUSCETTA
TO GIOVANNI BRUSCA

The wall of silence begins to crumble: one of the Mafia trials conducted by the judiciary of Reggio Calabria. It was not until 2000 that prosecutors were able to obtain convictions for the illegal rackets managed by the clans in the port of Gioia Tauro.

The pentiti rebel against the increasingly merciless laws of the Mafia, turning on the bosses and corrupt politicians who had protected them. Tommaso Buscetta confesses all about the structure of the Mafia and the involvement of public institutions at the highest level. Giovanni Brusca reveals the principal players and those behind the scenes of the attack on Judge Giovanni Falcone.

The Wall of *Omertà* Begins to Crumble

To break the wall of *omertà*, the ironclad law of silence with which the Mafia protects itself, is to invite a death sentence. The authorities have crashed up against this wall of silence ever since their arrival in Sicily in 1861 with the creation of the Kingdom of Italy. It would take more than one hundred years and dozens of trials (most of which would end in acquittal due to "insufficient evidence") before the Sicilian Mafia would be hit hard from within. In fact, it was only with the so-called maxi-trial that began in Palermo on February 10, 1986, that the organization really reached a crisis. The primary [1] evidence in that trial was provided by the *pentito* Tommaso Buscetta to Giovanni Falcone, Paolo Borsellino, and the other judges from the anti-Mafia pool, whose inquest involving 707 people and 1,314 interrogations led to the successful indictment of 475 defendants. A first verdict was handed down on December 16, 1987, and, at the request of public prosecutors Giuseppe Ayala and Domenico Signorino, it brought almost four hundred convictions for a total of 2,665 years

in prison, in addition to the nineteen life sentences given to people such as Totò Riina and Bernardo Provenzano, who were in hiding at the time.[2]

The verdict was confirmed for a third and final time by the first division of the Italian Court of Cassation (similar to a supreme court), at the time presided over by Giuseppe Di Gennaro, the future anti-Mafia super-prosecutor. In earlier years that division of the court had tried and often acquitted, in coordination with other judges, several defendants accused of Mafia-related crimes. This court was the subject of furious press scrutiny because of its alleged complicity with organized crime.[3] If the maxi-trial of 1986 was characterized mainly by the decisive contribution of the *pentiti* after years of unsatisfactory results in the courts, it must also be said that the phenomenon of the *pentito*, and more generally of betrayal from inside the organization, was nothing new.

A History of Betrayal

Incidents of the first breaks in *omertà* are almost as old as the Sicilian Mafia itself. By the middle of the nineteenth century, police reports were full of information on the activities, alliances, crimes, and disputes of the various families that shared control of the island, indicating that the organization was not as solid or as tight-knit as it might seem from the outside. This material came from police informers who acted as spies, and also from those known by the mafiosi as *'nfami* (Sicilian for wicked or infamous). These figures were pushed to cooperate with the authorities either for money or as a way of taking revenge. One such who betrayed the Mafia code of silence was Giuseppa Di Sano. In 1896,

Left: Lawyers and journalists during one of the maxi-trial hearings against the mafia, which took place in Palermo in 1986.

Facing Page: When the truth drives one mad. Leonardo Vitale, a soldier in the gangs, accused Totò Riina and Vito Ciancimino, the mayor of Palermo, of Mafia activity. He was declared insane and sent to a criminal psychiatric hospital. Other mafiosi actually resorted to this stratagem in order to avoid a prison sentence.

following the murder of her daughter, she put investigators on the trail of those responsible for the crime. As the investigators discovered, the true target of the gangs was Giuseppa herself, wrongly believed to be a police informer, and to deserve a death sentence for revealing the existence of a counterfeiting operation.[4] If she hadn't been an informer previously, the actions of the Mafia forced her to become one.

Such "betrayals" might also result from being in the wrong place at the wrong time, which happened to a young shepherd named Giuseppe Letizia in 1948. He had the misfortune to witness the murder of a man on the Busambra estate, and the even worse luck of not being able to keep quiet about it, particularly as the man in question was labor leader Placido Rizzotto, assassinated by Luciano Leggio on orders from Mafia boss and local doctor Michele Navarra. Some say[5] that same local doctor arranged for the boy to be killed with a lethal injection when he had been taken to the hospital for treatment for shock.

Signs of Repentance Among Men of Honor

The first cracks in the wall of *omertà* began to be seen in the mid-1970s. On March 30, 1973, Leonardo Vitale, a "soldier" on the lower rungs of the organization suspected of kidnapping, was struck by a true "mystical crisis,"[6] and of his own accord decided to present himself at the local police station. Vitale had a lot to say. He described the initiation rite of the Mafia, which up until that time had been described in almost surreal narratives in the mythology of the organization. He spoke of the "tests of courage" given to someone who wanted to join, and told how he was able to pass the test only on the second attempt, by killing a *campiere* in the town of Altarello-Porta Nuova who did not wish to submit to the authority of the local Mafia. (Vitale had failed his first test because he did not have the stomach to pull the trigger of a 12-gauge shotgun on a horse that was grazing in a field.) Vitale's "repentance" was marked by behavior that was almost delirious. It was caused, he said in documents collected after his death by the inquest of the maxi-trial of 1986, by the sin "of having been born in, and living in, a society where everyone is a mafioso, and for that reason is respected, while anyone who is not a mafioso is scorned."[7] A society, he added, "in which I remained a victim, I, Leonardo Vitale, who has risen in the faith of the true God." The first judges did not take these revelations seriously and Vitale was considered mad and sent to a mental hospital. Released in June 1984, he was murdered by the Mafia on December 2 of that year as he was leaving Mass with his family.

In May 1978, Giuseppe Di Cristina, the Sicilian boss of the town of Riesi, decided to turn himself in to the police in an attempt to block the expansionist aims of the Corleonesi, who were led by Luciano Leggio, Totò Riina, and Bernardo Provenzano. Di Cristina supplied the police with details of the murderous groups that had ordered the elimination of members of his own clan, thereby hoping to use the authorities to curb his rivals' excessive power. Just a few days later he was killed on a street in Palermo.

Only a few years later, however, that wall of silence began to collapse completely, even in the halls of justice. It had already been undermined by confidences and pieces of information shared in police stations and entrusted to that "personal and necessarily ambiguous"[8] relationship which existed between certain mafiosi and the authorities. This marked a crucial change in Mafia culture, as was illustrated most clearly by the Palermo maxi-trial. The trial signaled the onset of a period in which mafiosi began to speak in open court, and to violate in public their own code of silence. In addition to the decision by certain men of honor

to collaborate with the law, and the use of more sophisticated investigative methods shared between departments, this qualitative leap in the fight against organized crime was also helped by the introduction of important new legislation.

The Law Sets a Trap from within the Organization

The term "mafia" would not appear in any official documents of the Italian Republic until 1975. It took another seven years, with the approval of a law proposed by a member of Parliament from Sicily, Pio La Torre, for the penal code to acknowledge the specific crime of belonging to a mafia-style criminal organization. La Torre was killed by the Mafia in 1982 before the law was passed. The new law enabled judges to overcome the difficulties regarding rules of evidence that, among other factors, had given the bosses and their subordinates substantial immunity from prosecution. Up until then, in order to convict criminals associated with the gangs, the judges could use only the more general charge of association for the purpose of committing a crime. That was difficult to apply to a complex organization such as the Mafia and also required proof of the group's specific objectives. In short, it required proof of the existence of a gang and then assigning responsibility for its crimes to those belonging to it. With the new article 416a of the penal code, those procedural obstacles were overcome. Crucially, the article accepted as proven the existence of a mafia-style organization any time a group of at least three persons, making use of intimidation and imposing a condition of subjugation and silence on its members, committed

crimes for any of the following purposes: managing and controlling economic assets; the granting of concessions and authorizations to obtain contracts, public services, profits, and unfair advantages for itself or others; and the prevention or obstruction of the free exercise of the right to vote for the purpose of influencing political elections. Armed with a precise legal definition of the Mafia and its activities, the judges in the Palermo maxi-trial now stood a fighting chance against the organization.

Tommaso Buscetta Drops a Bombshell

The last of seventeen children, Tommaso Buscetta was born in Palermo on July 13, 1928, to a family of humble origin. He began to engage in illegal activities while still a teenager and had joined the Mafia by the age of seventeen, where he was nicknamed Don Masino. At the end of the World War II he moved to South America, to the cities of Buenos Aires and Rio de Janeiro, where he tried to go into business, but with poor results. He returned to Palermo in 1950 and in the following decade became close to the La Barbera clan. Their activities included tobacco smuggling, but they

would soon run up against the ruthless Corleonesi gang. During the 1960s, when the first conflict between rival gangs covered Sicily with blood, Buscetta went on the run and moved between the United States, Brazil, and Mexico under a false identity. Arrested for the first time in 1972 by the Brazilian police, he was extradited to Italy and sentenced to eight years in prison for drug trafficking. Upon his release in 1980, Buscetta returned to South America, perhaps because he felt that he was threatened. His proximity to families targeted by the Corleonesi had become dangerous for his closest relatives, too, as was evident by the disappearance of Benedetto and Antonio, two of the four children from his first marriage, in 1982 and 1984, during the second Mafia war. That was only the first of the "indirect" vendettas that would strike Buscetta's brother, brother-in-law, son-in-law, and four nephews.

On October 24, 1983, Buscetta was arrested in Sao Paulo and, knowing that the Brazilian authorities intended to hand him over to the Italians, he attempted suicide by swallowing strychnine. The press gave maximum coverage to the arrest of "the boss of two worlds," although

His fate is decided. Buscetta, pictured here surrounded by carabinieri after his extradition from Brazil, was in 1984 more or less forced to become a "collaborator with justice," telling the authorities everything he knew in order to take revenge on the Mafia.

Buscetta's involvement with the two groups was unusual and in clear contrast to the strict separation that existed, even in the upper reaches of the hierarchy, between the Cosa Nostra in America and the Mafia in Sicily. Helpless in the face of the gangs that had crushed those dearest to him, and persuaded by Judge Giovanni Falcone, Tommaso Buscetta agreed to collaborate with the authorities during the summer of 1984, providing the prosecutors with the foundations on which they could build the maxi-trial. "I declare at the start," he said in the initial testimony given to the investigators, "that I am not a sneak, in the sense that what I am going to say will not be said for the purpose of gaining the favor of the authorities. And neither am I a *pentito*, in the sense that my revelations are not offered out of base calculation"[9] on grounds of expediency. Buscetta did not deny his past and was explicit in his revelations, including details about the initiation rite involving the burning of a saint's card to symbolize the "death of a normal man and his rebirth" as a man of honor.[10] This new man is considered to have entered forever into a *sottomondo,* or "underworld," governed by rules and morals the opposite of those of the *sovramondo,* or "upper world", of official institutions. In this sense, Buscetta was the one who felt betrayed by a Mafia that had failed to uphold its promised social order as a true and proper "state within the state." He felt fooled by a Mafia that, in his opinion, had been irremediably compromised by systematic violence motivated exclusively by one group seeking to impose its supremacy over everyone else, at whatever cost and by whatever means.

A Journey Inside the Structure of the Mafia

Buscetta turned to the authorities because he had been defeated by his enemies, as had Giuseppe Di Cristina. But even in his new role as collaborator, Buscetta retained the typical sensibility of a mafioso in that he tried to continue the battle by using his agreement with the *sovramondo* as a weapon against his enemies and as a means of revenge. He revealed the structure of the Mafia, explaining precisely how in Palermo the men of honor belonged to a particular district, known in the small towns as a *località*, or territory, under the control of a specific family. The family was ruled by a boss elected with the consent of the other members. He in turn chose a *sottocapo,* or underboss, one or more *consiglieri*, or advisors, and several *capo decina*, or crew leaders (i.e., "boss of ten"), whose job it was to coordinate the activities of the ten soldiers under his command. According to Buscetta, at the top of the Mafia pyramid, above the families, there was a collective body known as the Commission made of representatives of the various neighboring Mafia clans. At the head of the Commission was the *Padrino* dei padrini*, or "godfather of godfathers." He in turn was in contact with people at higher levels who operated in secret and were in collusion with still others at the very highest level of government. There was, in other words, a third level, about which Buscetta refused to speak. The Mafia Commission, also known as the "Cupola," was centralized, and acted as a kind of board of directors to decide which crimes could be carried out by the Mafia. No crime could be committed without their authorization, whether "serious" crimes against magistrates, policemen, and politicians, or murders of "lesser" mafiosi, which still required permission from the clan ruling the area in which the crime was to be committed. Starting with the maxi-trial, the existence of this "Cupola" allowed the authorities to assign criminal responsibility almost automatically to anyone who had been either part of it, or a member of one of the families represented on it. After his revelations to the Italian authorities, Tommaso Buscetta was extradited to the United States, where he received a new identity and, in exchange for further information about the American Cosa Nostra, probation. He died of a serious illness at the age of seventy-two in New York on April 2, 2000.

Collaborators in revenge. Francesco Marino Mannoia followed Buscetta's example after the murder of his brother. The Corleone gang tried to stop his confessions by killing members of his family, but in vain.

The Other *Pentiti*

Following Buscetta's confessions there was a veritable flood of *pentiti*, of both lesser and greater prominence, eager to break the conspiratorial silence that surrounded the Mafia. Bloodcurdling stories emerged attesting to the groups' ruthlessness, with one witness confirming the existence of Mafia death chambers in which enemies of the clan were killed and then dissolved in acid. Some were prompted by personal tragedy, such as Francesco Marino Mannoia, whose mother, sister, and aunt were all murdered by the Mafia in an attempt to intimidate him. "Are you aware," he asked Falcone, "of how much strength is needed to strangle a man? Do you realize that it can take ten minutes? And that the victim writhes, bites, and kicks? Some even succeed in freeing themselves from the rope. But at least the killing

is done by a professional."[11] At the end of his statement he accused the Corleonesi, who had shattered the gangs' territorial equilibrium with unprecedented savagery, of perhaps the most heinous crime of all: unprofessionalism.

In 1991 the phenomenon of "repentance" was made more frequent by another legislative measure passed by the Italian parliament. It applied to organized crime measures analogous to those used to defeat political terrorism during the 1980s. The new law established rules for the "collaborator with justice" (*collaboratore di giustizia*, the legal term for a person popularly known as a *pentito*). Among other things, it provided for reduced sentences in exchange for useful information, as well as specific guidelines for the protection of another category of witness, the *testimone di giustizia** ("witness of justice"). While the *pentito* is a criminal, often cooperating in exchange for a reduced prison sentence, the *testimone di giustizia* is not a criminal but is part of the Mafia underworld nonetheless, perhaps through a family connection, or through

the sheer misfortune of being in the wrong place at the wrong time. Such witnesses require specific protection: a new identity and sufficient economic support to remove them from their normal environment and protect them from revenge. Seventeen-year-old Rita Atria was such a witness. She turned to Judge Paolo Borsellino for the arrest of the murderers of her father and brother, killed in the Corleonesi's Mafia war. Following the trial she lived in secret in Rome, as provided by the witness protection program, ostracized by her own mother for breaking the code, and with only her police protectors for companionship. She committed suicide on July 26, 1992, one week after Borsellino lost his life.

"This Is How I Killed Judge Giovanni Falcone"

Guilty by his own admission of more than one hundred and fifty crimes,[12] Giovanni Brusca, born in San Giuseppe Jato, Sicily, in 1957, was captured by the police on May 20, 1996. The agents surprised him at home while he was watching a television documentary about the massacre of Judge Giovanni Falcone. The decision by Brusca to become a *pentito* was not immediate; after all, following the arrest of Totò Riina, Brusca had become leader of the merciless Corleonesi clan in a deal with Bernardo Provenzano. But Brusca later decided to collaborate with the authorities and confessed to, among other things, his personal participation in what he described as some of the "first-rate killings" that had covered Palermo in blood. He admitted to detonating the bomb that killed Judge Rocco Chinnici and his escort, and to

ordering the kidnappers who were holding fifteen-year-old Giuseppe Di Matteo hostage to strangle him and dissolve his body in acid as a means of punishing his father Santino. He also provided some of the first revelations about the fatal attack on Judge Falcone. According to Brusca, that attack had already been approved by the higher-ups in the Mafia at the end of 1982, but it was postponed

in order to resolve—with Kalashnikovs—problems within the organization itself. Falcone's murder served to "eliminate him and all our adversaries . . . those who were first our friends and have now become our enemies . . . I refer in particular to men in politics . . . for example those who carried out everything that Falcone himself wanted: his laws, his provisions, his restrictive measures."[13] Brusca's conviction had been foreseen for some time but was carried out in the most sensational way only in the summer of 1992 (see "The Position of the Catholic Church", p. 157).

Giovanni Brusca was known as a *scannacristiani*, which roughly means "someone who cuts the throat of Christians." In Sicilian dialect, "Christian" means a human being, and in Mafia slang the term

A killer pentito in semi-custody. Giovanni Brusca committed the massacre at Capaci and ordered the murder of young Giuseppe Di Matteo, who was dissolved in acid, among other crimes. In 2004, thanks to his confessions, his prison sentence was served under more lenient conditions.

Mafia messages. Graffiti on the wall of a house on the border between the towns of San Cipirello and San Giuseppe Jato that appeared after Brusca's arrest and his almost immediate decision to collaborate with the authorities. The reference to 18 karats was meant to raise the question on whether his repentance was genuine.

is synonymous with "man of honor."[14] Brusca's job was literally that of a cutthroat, i.e., to punish mafiosi who had become enemies. Although the Italian law on *pentiti* was modified in 2001 and was more restrictive than the original 1991 law, it still preserved the right to a lesser sentence (no more than one-fourth of the original sentence) and to the granting of a maintenance allowance by the government, both of which Brusca was able to benefit from. These new rules had been devised to avoid the phenomenon of "false repentance" and to hinder unverifiable revelations made only for the purpose of serving a shorter sentence.

Some officials thought the new rules risked weakening the pressure that could be exerted on someone inclined to cooperate. For example, a *pentito* has a maximum of six months from the time he begins his cooperation in which to tell everything that he knows, despite the fact that events often go back many years and it may be difficult to remember everything in detail. His benefits begin only after his statements are evaluated and judged to be significant and new, while the protection afforded him by the authorities stops when the danger of reprisal and revenge is no longer present, without any consideration of the length of time in which the information provided to the investigators is used. Thanks to the rules of 2004, Brusca received special permission from the court to leave prison for short periods every forty-five days in order to

visit his family, with a maximum of two months between one visit and the next. The episode served to once more stir up the polemics between those who supported the need to encourage *pentiti* with very precise exceptions to the law and those who felt that the existing laws were an indispensable tool in the fight against organized crime and should not be modified, particularly not to the benefit of the *pentiti*.

Implacable justice. In the mid-1990s John Paul II condemned the Mafia in the strongest terms during his visit to Sicily.

THE POSITION OF THE CATHOLIC CHURCH

For many, the notion of "repentance" is inextricably linked with religion, and it is interesting to consider the position of the Catholic Church regarding the Mafia. Cardinal Ernesto Ruffini was the first member of the clergy to address the issue officially, in a pastoral letter published in 1964.[1] His analysis of the phenomenon, although it was consistent with current ideas about the Mafia, appeared to many commentators, even of later periods as being too lenient, even for a man of the cloth. According to Ruffini, "if it is true that the term Mafia is of local origin, specifically from Sicily, it is also true that the reality which the term implies exists more or less everywhere, and perhaps elsewhere to a worse degree." More explicit condemnation of the Mafia would come from Ruffini's successor, Cardinal Salvatore Pappalardo, during a sermon given in 1982 on the occasion of the funeral of General Carlo Alberto Dalla Chiesa and his wife Emanuela Setti Carraro, murdered by the Mafia in a hail of bullets. "While the government in Rome holds debates, Sagunto, that is, Palermo, is vanquished," said Pappalardo from the pulpit. It would also come from Pope John Paul II during his trip to Sicily in November 1995 "I cannot help but repeat," he said in his pastoral address in Palermo, "the cry that pours out from my heart: Do not kill. No man, no association of men, no Mafia can change or crush underfoot the right to life. This most sacred right comes from God." Priests Don Giuseppe Puglisi, murdered in 1993, and Don Peppino Diana, struck by the bullets of the Neapolitan Camorra in 1994, had already paid for such judgments with their lives.

1. Vincenzo Ceruso, *Le sagrestie di Cosa Nostra* (Rome: Newton Compton editori, 2007), 152.

THE FINANCIAL
ORGANIZATION OF THE MAFIA

How the Mafia finances itself, from arms trafficking to public contracts to the illegal disposal of waste. The Mafia and the international markets: money laundering and the era of the white-collar Mafia investments.

A Financial Journey: from Las Vegas to Switzerland

In 1965 the FBI obtained the first tangible evidence that a substantial part of the Mafia's profits from its casinos in Las Vegas was being transferred to bank accounts in Switzerland. Amazingly, it was all due to chance: a receipt, found in a parking lot at Miami airport, showed the transfer of some three hundred and fifty thousand dollars to a Geneva bank[1] belonging to a Canadian citizen resident in Lausanne, who had been arrested in 1931 for selling liquor during Prohibition. Investigators were able to establish that it referred to a business associate of Meyer Lansky, the former right-hand man of Lucky Luciano and a prominent member of the Cosa Nostra who was

now the financial brains behind the organization. The receipt had been lost by a courier who transported suitcases with the daily take from the Las Vegas casinos, which came to something like 1 million dollars a month—undeclared to the Inland Revenue Service. Some of that went directly to Mafia families, but the largest part was sent out of the country through branches of obliging banks in Miami and the Bahamas, and ended up in Switzerland. The FBI suspected that the profits earned by the Mafia in the casinos, along with its profits from prostitution and drug trafficking, were laundered through a complicated series of transactions in order to conceal its illicit origins. By the end of the 1960s it amounted to tens of millions of dollars a year, which, once it

Top: Calculated risk. Gambling has always been one of the main sources of funding for criminal organizations. Between 1950 and 1960, the Cosa Nostra used the cover of casinos in Las Vegas, to launder huge sums of money in the legal economy.

Bottom: The prostitution racket has grown enormously in recent years, above all on the roads of southern Europe. Its development is also due to the increase in immigrants from Eastern Europe, which began with the collapse of communism.

had arrived overseas would then be sent back to the United States to be invested in operations managed by apparently legitimate businessmen, including the acquisition, on behalf of the bosses, of large amounts of real estate in Florida, New York, and California. Moreover, hidden transfers of wealth, first to Switzerland and Liechtenstein and then permanently to other countries in Europe as well as the Cayman Islands and Hong Kong—or to any country that protects banking secrecy—allowed the criminal organizations to obstruct investigations concerning their funds in the countries of origin.

However, in 1970 a new law was passed in the United States for the purposes of fighting organized crime. The snappily named RICO act (the Racketeer Influenced and Corrupt Organizations act, but also named for the main character in the Al Capone inspired film *Little Caesar*) passed a law that allowed prosecutors to indict Mafia bosses regardless of their actual participation in a specific crime, as had been required in the past. They could now be held accountable for every crime committed by the criminal enterprises of which they were the leaders, including murder, robbery, drug trafficking, gambling, prostitution, and fraud. RICO permitted the confiscation of assets acquired through criminal activity, including houses and other properties, and bank accounts.[2] These provisions aimed to destroy the economic foundations that supported the criminal underworld, which was forced to employ ever more refined strategies to escape prosecution.

Undercover Financial Operations: The Mafia and the Banks of Michele Sindona

During the 1980s, the American Cosa Nostra and the Sicilian Mafia were at the center of a financial scandal with a network so complex it was never completely understood by the judicial authorities investigating it, but it was believed to have stretched as far as the Istituto per le Opere Religiose, more commonly known as the Vatican Bank. One of the key players in the drama was Michele Sindona, a Sicilian financier with close connections with the New York Mafia, who specialized in money laundering. Sindona was born in Sicily in 1920, and had maintained his contacts there ever since. He was looked on by the Mafia as a clever business manager able to facilitate contacts between the Cosa Nostra and the influential sectors in Italy, such as politicians and Freemasons, who wanted to make use of the gangs' control of electoral votes in the fight against Communism. Sindona could also manage the flow of money generated by drug trafficking and arms sales.[3]

Such a business was risky. Roberto Calvi, a Milanese banker who moved in those same circles, came to a mysterious end: his body was discovered in London on June 18, 1982, hanging from Blackfriars Bridge above the Thames. There were bricks in his pockets and some fifteen thousand dollars. The verdict of the British authorities was suicide, but several judicial inquiries in Italy have suggested his death was linked to that complicated interweaving of illegal transactions and political-criminal interests that also engulfed Sindona.

Roberto Calvi (on the left with moustache), a Milanese financier known as "God's Banker," was at the center of a sensational financial scandal in the early 1980s. Implicated in the collapse of Banco Ambrosiano, one of the main Italian Catholic banks, and accused of following the interests of the Mafia and other obscure powers, Calvi was found hanged from Blackfriars Bridge in London in June 1982.

Sindona overcome his humble background thanks to his great aptitude for mathematics. This had enabled him to acquire a number of banks by the late 1960s, through which he was able to move large sums of money. According to statements made by *pentiti*, Sindona was the financial manager for the Sicilian Mafia, who facilitated their secret contacts with officials in government. But by 1974 the banks controlled by this great wheeler-dealer began to have problems, and suffered from a financial crash known as Il Crack Sindona. Because of this, the criminal groups demanded their money back. In his attempt to save himself from the American authorities, Sindona staged a fake kidnapping to allow him to return secretly to Sicily, where he attempted to collect the enormous sums of money demanded by his creditors. The authorities were on to him by this time, but Sindona continued to evade justice, while those who attempted to stop him were often violently punished: a lawyer given the task of liquidating Sindona's banks, Giorgio Ambrosoli, was found murdered in Milan in July 1979, a crime for which Sindona was extradited from the United States to Italy, and sentenced to life in prison for instigating. On March 22, 1986, in the maximum-security prison at Voghera in the Italian province of Lombardy, Sindona died from drinking coffee laced with poison.

Mafia financiers on trial. Michele Sindona had an important role in the management of Mafia finances in Italy and the United States, and in links between the organization and the worlds of politics and freemasonry. He was poisoned in prison and took his secrets to the grave.

New Criminal Power and the Business Turnover of the 'Ndrangheta

The brutal attacks on Giovanni Falcone and Paolo Borsellino in 1992 exposed the Sicilian Mafia to sustained retaliation by the authorities, culminating in the arrests of Totò Riina in 1993 and Bernardo Provenzano in 2006. The intense investigative activity that was focused on those two bosses was partly responsible for diverting the authorities away from other criminal organizations southern Italy.[4] The Calabrian 'Ndrangheta, for example, was now able to exert its authority far from its home region, as the massacre at Duisburg, Germany, in August 2007 illustrated.

The name 'Ndrangheta refers to the blood ties that unite those entire families (known in Calabria as *n'drine*) who engage in illegal activities. No other criminal organization is characterized by bonds of kinship as close as those of the Calabrian 'Ndrangheta. These bonds are so deeply rooted and so conditioned by the identification of each member with his clan that the phenomenon of the *pentito* is virtually unknown. However, the often age-old quarrels between families result in a chain of endless vendettas. It is, wrote Paolo Borsellino, an organization that operates with the same method of "intimidation and violence as the Sicilian Mafia" but does not have that organization's "oligarchic and unitary" structure,[5] i.e., the Commission, or board of directors capable of coordinating its activities. However, its ability to control a mountainous territory almost unreachable by the authorities, and thanks in part to the complicity of the local population, led the 'Ndrangheta to exploit kidnappings as a way to accumulate enormous riches.

Among the abductions organized by the gangs during the 1980s, the kidnapping of Cesare Casella aroused particular attention. He was abducted at the age of eighteen in the city of Pavia in northern Italy on January 18, 1988, and released after 743 days in captivity on January 30, 1990, in the town of Natile di Careri in Calabria. The ransom paid was equivalent to about eight hundred thousand dollars. But it was not the money paid out by his family that secured Cesare's freedom: it was the public outcry roused by the courage of his mother, who personally went to the piazzas and churches of the region to plead for the release of her son and to press for more decisive action by the state against such a barbaric custom. Shortly afterwards, legislation was passed allowing the Italian judiciary to block the assets of the victim's family, making kidnapping far less financially attractive for the 'Ndrangheta. Because of this, in 1990, they became involved in other areas of criminal activity, such as arms trafficking, or the management of public contracts obtained through corrupt local politicians. These included electric power plants, airport infrastructure, and telecommunications, as well as illegal construction near beaches and well-known tourist resorts. The 'Ndrangheta infiltrated the lucrative drugs trade, too, eventually reaching the top levels of international drug trafficking.[6] An increasingly borderless Europe made it ever easier for the Calabrian gangs to penetrate other countries, as seen both by the events in Duisburg and by the fact that they now have a presence in nineteen countries on four continents.

A Business Model Made for Export

The 'Ndrangheta, like the Sicilian Mafia, has first-class financial experts at its disposal, uses laptops to manage the traffic of drugs and to move huge fortunes from one boss to another in different parts of the world, and knows everything about the new technologies that enable it to avoid telephone intercepts. But its main strength is its ability to adapt to the environment in which it wishes to operate. In Italy, the Calabrian gangs are suspected of having laundered the proceeds of their activities in Rome, through the purchase of formerly exclusive resorts. In Germany, on the other hand, the 'Ndrangheta has set up an extensive network of pizzerias in order to provide legal cover for the sale of cocaine. It has also, as verified by the Bundesnachrichtendienst, the German intelligence services, invested millions of dollars in shares in hotel chains and restaurants in the east of the country, all of which demonstrates its ability to move with confidence and fewer difficulties than in its own country. One of the reasons for this is German law: in Germany it is illegal to subject suspects to wiretapping in public places and money laundering is relatively easy because there is no obligation to prove to the banks that the money invested comes from legitimate sources. Also, and unlike in Italy, in Germany the crime of belonging to a criminal organization does not exist, and prosecutors

Seven hundred and forty-three days away from home. Cesare Casella, victim of one of the longest kidnappings in the history of Italian organized crime, wrote a book about his experience as a 'Ndrangheta prisoner.

are therefore obliged to prove the accused was planning a specific crime before being able to proceed with the preventive seizure of goods.[7]

The Neapolitan Camorra and the Arrival of the Eco-Mafia

Nothing but a vague memory remains of the Bella Società Riformata, a criminal organization active in the working-class neighborhoods of Naples in the late nineteenth century.[8] But it is to that sect, inspired by secret revolutionary brotherhoods active in sixteenth-century Spain, that we owe the spread of the Camorra in Campania, in the nineteenth century.

The origin of the Neapolitan group's name is subject to a great deal of conjecture and conflicting theories. In Spanish, for instance, *camorra* means a brawl or a quarrel, and a *camorrista* is an argumentative person. Yet the word also resembles the Arabic *gumuria* meaning "republic," and is perhaps testament to the influence of Arabic on Spanish during the time of Muslim rule. It was certainly a republic of

crime that the Bella Società Riformata imposed on Naples, by force and through extortion. There is another theory with origins closer to home: according to a nineteenth-century Neapolitan-Tuscan dictionary, *camorra* was a synonym for *pizzo*, or protection money, the "tax" imposed on small businesses in the area.

Unlike its secretive predecessor, the Camorra was clearly visible to the populace. In order to show its courage as well as its brutality, its members, even into the twentieth century, would challenge each other in public to duels. These duels were similar to those engaged in by the aristocracy (and, indeed, Neapolitan slang for duel, *zumpate*, refers to the lunge in fencing) but with one substantial difference: replacing the aristocratic rapier as the duelists' weapon of choice was a knife.

The Camorra differs from the Sicilian Mafia in terms of its geographic reach and its "horizontal" character, in contrast to the pyramidal structure of the both the Sicilian and American Mafias. In 1970, the powerful Camorra boss Raffaele Cutolo tried to create a more functional and well-structured framework for sharing the territory. He founded the New Camorra and set down in writing the initiation rites for members, which drew from those of the ancient sect from Spain. Cutolo was unsuccessful in creating a single coordinating structure similar to that of the Sicilian Commission, but he would efficiently manage illegal activities, including drug trafficking, arms sales, kidnapping, extortion, and the theft of long-distance trucks. One of the most profitable trades was in contraband cigarettes, brought in by sea and smuggled on to ships anchored along the coasts. Tobacco smuggling in more recent years has shifted to Puglia. It has also become one of the most profitable activities for the Sacra Corona Unita, another criminal organization with rites and methods of operation very similar to those of the 'Ndrangheta.

In recent years the center of criminal activity in the Campania region moved to the province of Caserta. There, in the town of Casal di Principe, the Casalesi clan became dominant over others in the area. What was formerly settled with a duel on a country road has today given way to ruthless executions of adversaries carried out in broad daylight. The local bosses soon began to operate on a national level and made investments in agricultural businesses in Umbria, hotels in Tuscany, and nightclubs in Emilia Romagna. Their interests extended to the real estate and supermarket sectors in the north of Italy, eventually entering Piazza Affari, the heart of high finance in Milan and home to the Italian stock exchange.[9]

The Illegal Traffic in Waste Material

The enormous profits generated by these illegal activities compelled the criminal organizations to find legal ways to invest their money. From the late 1980s to the present, an ever-more substantial part of those profits—especially in Campania, a region with severe environmental problems—was diverted to the traffic in waste material, the focus of the so-called "eco-Mafia*." Trash also became big business for the Casalesi clan. In its territory it

Left: Charismatic leader. In the 1970s, boss Raffaele Cutolo transformed the Neapolitan Camorra into an industry of crime. He reunited the clans under his command, made alliances with the 'Ndrangheta from Calabria and used their old initiation rites. To finance the organization he even imposed a "tax" on contraband cigarettes.

Facing page, top: Drug trafficking. Seizures by the Italian police along the routes that run from South America and Turkey into the European narcotics market.

Bottom: Cigarette smuggling. Once the monopoly of the Neapolitan Camorra, the trade in contraband cigarettes is now run by Albanian clans in close contact with the Sacra Corono Unita of Puglia.

controlled hundreds of garbage dumps, both legal and illegal, in addition to dozens of businesses specializing in the disposal of hazardous industrial waste, such as the toxic phosphorous pentaflouride. According to environmental groups who have studied the issue, over the last ten years the eco-Mafia has collected around 200 billion dollars from the illegal management of toxic waste. Ever-closer inspections by the authorities, and the discovery of ever-larger areas in which drums containing waste were simply buried, with no regard for the laws that require their safe storage and, where possible, their recycling, did not prevent the clans from finding new sites in which to hide the waste. They continued to profit from the activity, benefiting from the lower costs of illegal disposal compared to the costs incurred by plants that observed the environmental laws. Where they could not exploit illegal dumping, the gangs imposed a *pizzo* for the legal disposal of refuse, demanding a kickback in exchange for permits granted by corrupt politicians. This phenomenon of the "eco-Mafia" spread, with similar arrangements,

Nuova Camorra
Organizzata
(New Organized
Camorra). Raffaele
Cutolo was planning
on creating a
pyramid structure
for Camorra, similar
to that of the Mafia.
Put on trial several
times, he feigned
insanity to receive
lighter sentences.

to the 'Ndrangheta's territory in Calabria. In the northern Italy, businesses sought to save the cost of disposal by giving the gangs tens of thousands of cubic yards of waste full of lead, hydrocarbons, and chromium, which was either buried with the landowners' complicity or sent to China on container ships. These were often the same ships that had just unloaded cargoes of counterfeit merchandise intended for the European market, with unbeatable prices due to the use of low-cost labor in their countries of origin and from the evasion of customs duties. These ships now set sail again, full of poisons for their far-off destination.[10] It was a business worth billions. An investigation into its organization led, in 2009, to the discovery of an actual criminal agreement between gangs of the Calabrian 'Ndrangheta and the Chinese in the Italian port of Gioia Tauro, in the province of Reggio Calabria.[11]

In Russia, like in Italy: a "white-collar" mafia

According to a study made by the influential Italian research institute Eurispes, in 2008 organized crime had a turnover of some 250 billion dollars in Italy alone, while the influence exerted by criminal groups on the economy, society, and public institutions in the southern part of the country continued to grow.[12] The business interests of organized criminal groups constituted a genuine underground economy. The profits came from drug trafficking, prostitution, cigarette smuggling, fake goods, and the counterfeiting of bank notes, as well as from arms sales and the manipulation of public contracts. This underground economy also profited from loan-sharking and extortion as well as trafficking in illegal immigrants from North Africa headed for the coasts of Italy.

The rise of the Casalesi. After the imprisonment of Cutolo, control of many of the illegal activities carried out in Campania by the Nuova Camorra Organizzata (NCO) passed to other clans, like those in Casal di Principe. Arrests and investigations by the police have brought to light strong branches of these families in other regions throughout Italy.

The poison that oozes from waste abandoned in an illegal dump in Campania poisons crops and ground water.

The crisis that hit the international financial markets in September 2008, forced some one hundred and eighty thousand entrepreneurs to turn to usurers when they were unable to borrow money from legitimate banks. Moreover, Italian businessmen paid approximately 375 million dollars to organized crime in order to guarantee protection from the rackets, even in more financially fortunate places in northern Italy like Milan.[13] This picture now encompassed the global economy and seemed destined to become worse due to the spread of organized crime into developing countries and those of the former Soviet bloc.

The international spread of organized crime was able to exploit the profound geopolitical transformations of the last twenty years. In February, 1993, a Sicilian, together with a member of the American Mafia, acquired an international bank in southern Russia, based in a small village in the Urals, for an astonishing sum, and which was at the center of a military-industrial complex that provided equipment to the Russian army.

The spread of electronic networks has greatly facilitated the transfer and concealment of capital of illicit origin, despite the attempts by governments to pass ever more restrictive laws against the infiltration of the legal economy by organized crime. It is a truly difficult undertaking fighting this "white-collar" Mafia, one that now wears double-breasted suits and whose children are lawyers, businessmen, and experts in finance; a Mafia that wants to protect the new bosses from spending their lives in prison and safeguard its property from seizure.[14] In Italy, the fight against organized crime has in recent years resulted in an increase in the arrest of fugitives, along with a substantial increase in assets taken from the Mafia

clans (approximately 8 million dollars in 2008).[15] Only a fraction of these assets has been transferred to administrations and associations that later used the confiscated real estate to conduct legal activities, such as the production of foodstuffs. A more substantial part of these riches remains blocked by very complex legal procedures, which threaten, over time, to put these assets back in the hands of the very bosses from whom they were taken, through the use of straw men and obliging associates. In other countries, such as the United States, the federal agency for the management of assets, known as the Marshal Service, is in charge of managing property of illegal origin. It carries out confiscations in shorter periods of time than in Italy and puts those goods on the market for sale to the highest bidder, in the interests of all American taxpayers.[16]

Drug Sales and Arms Smuggling: The War Economies of the Mafia in Central Asia

Information contained in the 2009 annual report of the United Nations Office on Drugs and Crime provided fresh proof of the existence of an unusual correlation between the market for opium and the price of weapons in the wartime economy of Afghanistan. The research organization actually demonstrated that along with a substantial reduction of 22% in the acreage of poppy fields dedicated to the cultivation of the opium from which heroin is refined (approximately 300,000 acres, worth between 100 and 400 million dollars, part of which went to the guerrilla

Top: Environmental emergency. In Nola, toxic waste under the motorway that leads to Villa Literno, Campania. In 2008 the Italian authorities sent in the army to bring the situation back to normal.

Bottom: Investigations by the authorities have brought to light links between eco-Mafia groups active in southern Italy and other criminal organizations at an international level.

fighters), there was also a real boom in the price of AK-47 assault rifles made by Russia. The large reduction in the amount of opium produced in Central Asia was, according to other sources in the United Nations, the result of the "offensive" conducted in the region by the Food Zone project. It provided alternative seeds for planting and supported the sale of agricultural products by peasants who were willing to promise not to grow opium poppies. But according to the United Nations Office on Drugs and Crime, the reduced poppy cultivation was the result of a deliberate choice and closely connected to the increase in the cost of weapons. Ever since 2004, Afghanistan had been producing much more opium than the market could absorb. The ensuing collapse in the price of heroin would actually have pushed the local clans to cut back on production in order to bring supply and demand back into balance and thus avoid any risk that the markets might be inundated with heroin at bargain prices. The smaller cash receipts provided by drug trafficking would have meanwhile been offset by an immediate doubling in the price quoted for an AK-47 rifle, which by then was being sold in the area for around six hundred dollars each. Was this in effect a genuine marketing plan applied to organized crime? If these were not just random price fluctuations, completely free of outside influence, then one must ask whether the uppermost levels of the local criminal organizations were not receiving their instructions from business managers produced by the most prestigious business schools in the world.

The Confiscation of Mafia Treasure

In recent years, the fight against organized crime in Italy has led to the arrest of many godfathers who were on the run, and to a considerable increase in the confiscation of goods belonging to the gangs (some 15 billion dollars between April 2008 and May 2010[13]). Nevertheless, only some of the seized properties could be turned over to the government and used for legal activities. A large part of this wealth is still blocked by a very complex system of allocation of the sequestered goods, and it is a good bet that much will wind up right back in the lap of the Mafia thanks to the intervention of its various nominees and straw men. From 2010, the Italian government therefore decided to establish a system for administering seized assets that would be modeled on the United States Marshals Service, a Federal agency that manages assets confiscated as a result of illegal activity and which sells them with minimum delay to the highest bidder, all in the interest of the American taxpayer[14].

Poppy-growing in Asia. International organizations for cooperation in development have launched various initiatives to promote the reversion to agricultural production other than of opium.

THE **INTERNATIONAL** MAFIAS, FROM THE **JAPANESE** YAKUZA TO THE **RUSSIAN** AND **CHINESE** MAFIAS

The Mafia way of doing business spreads around the world. A comparison between the Mafia and criminal organizations in other countries: an analysis of their structures, interests, and methods of operation.

Ancient dynasties. Many criminal organizations, including those in Japan, confuse their own criminal origins with myth and legend. Some say that the ancestors of the Yakuza were samurais of the final shogun dynasty from the seventeenth to nineteenth century, and soldiers in ancient Tokyo.

The Mafia Goes Global

The predominant characteristic of the Sicilian Mafia, ever since its beginnings, has not simply been that it is organized in a pyramidal structure, at the top of which is the Commission, which represents the clans and through which the bosses decide how territory is to be shared, and illegal activities apportioned among the various groups. This is also true of the American Cosa Nostra, which originated in Sicily and arrived in the United States as part of the flow of migration that left the island in waves starting in the late nineteenth century. The most distinguishing characteristic of the

Cosa Nostra—what sets it apart from other forms of criminal behavior that are no less dangerous—is its ability to infiltrate the world of politics and to collude with those at the highest levels of government. The American Mafia has, due to factors both historical and environmental, largely succeeded in becoming a true "state within the state." An organization international in scope, the Mafia has its own codes and tribunals, with a military arm capable of exerting crushing force. It is able to make illegal withdrawals of funds through extortion. It commits crimes in order to accumulate capital and, especially today, to carry out sophisticated financial operations. Thanks to its involvement at the highest levels of official institutions, the Mafia is sometimes able to exert strong influence on, and turn to its advantage, decisions by the government and its administrative apparatus, all as part of a mechanism of reciprocal advantage. From this perspective, the model employed by the Sicilian-American Mafia has, in a certain sense, set the standard for the world.[1]

There will always be criminal organizations, with historical roots either recent or more ancient, that in the tumultuous development of a globalized economy have perfected their own methods of penetrating markets, by capitalizing on the protection offered by their own governments. Today, this growth of riches—submerged and often concealed by the official respectability of organized crime groups that mingle with governments—has reached alarming proportions. According to estimates made by the

World Bank and the International Monetary Fund, at the beginning of this century the total value of illegal economic activity in terms of productive capacity represented some 20 to 25 percent of worldwide gross domestic product, and therefore of the entire world's capacity to generate wealth. In 2001,[2] according to the same statistical sources, financial transactions related to the laundering of money resulting from illegal activities amounted to between 2 and 5 percent of worldwide gross domestic product, with a value of around 1.5 trillion dollars.

Katana blows. Prints and frescoes from the seventeenth century tell how a sword, at least 24 inches long, issued to the warrior class of samurais of the period, was later used to resolve private conflicts. The weapon was held with two hands with the blade pointing upwards, and was a symbol of power, honor, and membership of the warrior social class.

The Yakuza: When the Samurai Laid Down Their Swords

The Japanese Yakuza*, also known as the Gokudo, is without doubt one of the criminal organizations that has secured a place for itself in the political sphere. The name comes from the pronunciation in Japanese of the numbers eight, nine, and three in sequence, "ya-ku-za." These numbers represent the lowest score in a Japanese card game called Oicho-Kabu, which was one of the earliest rackets to receive attention from criminal organizations in the Far East. As with the Sicilian-American Cosa Nostra, the origins

of the Yakuza are shrouded in myth and legend. Its origins appear to date to the seventeenth century, the result of a kind of institutional diaspora that in a period of deep political and social instability marked by incessant internal wars relegated many samurai, who until that moment had been firmly rooted in the political power structure, to the margins of Japanese society. These impoverished aristocrats gathered together in groups dedicated to the oppression of the population and are considered by some to be the precursors of the criminal system that gave birth to the Yakuza.

However, there is another theory that suggests the ancestors of the Japanese mafia are to be found in the rebellious bands of servants known as *machi-yakko,* who rose up to defend the oppressed social classes against their rulers. Likewise dedicated to illegal activities, by the eighteenth century they came together in ever larger and more powerful associations that earned their money from gambling and extortion. They became important enough to induce the government to use them as a means of repression against popular revolts, in exchange for which they received immunity and protection from the law for their illegal trafficking. By the end of the nineteenth century, people associated with the Yakuza had climbed to the highest positions in Japan. This allowed the clans to take part in political rivalries and thereby obtain favors in exchange for the intimidation of opposing parties, creating ever larger opportunities for profit.

The Allied occupation led by the United States at the end of World War II temporarily reduced the Yakuza's importance, although it quickly adapted to the change in circumstances. The Yakuza succeeded in obtaining control of building contracts for postwar reconstruction in exchange for keeping public order. In 1992, in an attempt to stem the organization's progressive rise, the Japanese government enacted a law that declared illegal all those associations that resorted to intimidation and violence in the pursuit of illicit ends. Despite the arrest of many members, the clans were soon able to create an alliance to continue its various businesses, especially prostitution, extortion, and the

popular Japanese games of chance. Their semi-legal origins and deep roots in the territory have given the Yakuza a kind of respectability that is acknowledged by the rest of the population, despite the hundreds of murders attributed to the groups that are part of it.

Mafia bosses in the Far East make no attempt to conceal their allegiance, traveling in luxury automobiles and flaunting the multicolored tattoos that are an identifying feature of their membership. The Yakuza has, moreover, infiltrated the worlds of high finance and real estate speculation. It has illegal operations in other Asian countries such as the Philippines, Indonesia, South Korea, China, and Mongolia, as well as roots in the Japanese community that came to the United States at the end of World War II.

The Collapse of the Soviet Union and the Development of the Russian Mafia

The globalization of organized crime, understood in terms of alliances between criminal groups and their collusion with those at the highest levels of government, received a further push with the collapse of the Soviet Union starting in the late 1980s. The breakup of the former Soviet republics led to the acquisition of vast sectors of the economy for private profit, which had already begun to emerge before the end of the regime. In this sense the Russian mafiosi who today mix their lives as successful businessmen with new types of criminal activity can be seen as benefiting from a situation analogous to the one in Sicily in the nineteenth century, by which vast landed estates were acquired by *gabellotti*, the caretakers of those estates. The Sicilian Mafia became entwined with the progressive expansion of this new kind of landowner, one that was dedicated to crime and to the abuse of power on those estates that had once been part of the island's great landed property.[3]

With due regard for differences in geography and structure, the Russian mafia today is also able to exploit an economic system characterized by the sudden transition from state to private ownership. In its attempts to conquer ever larger dominions, and thanks to the support and the power of the military intimidation at its disposal, the Russian Mafia (known in Russian as the afiya or the Organizatsya* [organization]) is active not only within its homeland but also in the Balkan countries where the Soviet Union formerly exercised its influence. In the final years of the Soviet dictatorship, industrialists, real estate operators, and builders were able to profit from the winds of change by buying up at ridiculously low prices manufacturing plants, mineral rights, and vast buildable tracts on the outskirts of the main cities. Through their links with organized crime, their interests dovetailed with other criminal activities, such as drug trafficking and the sale of weapons decommissioned from the former Soviet arsenal.

The progressive transition to a market economy attracted interest from foreign investors, mostly from the West, which in turn drew the attention of the Organizatsya. The Russian Mafia was able to exploit the instability of the system, both in terms of the riskiness of the investments themselves, and in terms of the personal security of the new foreign tycoons while in Russia. Thanks to its powerful supporters, the Russian Mafia was able to meet the demand for security from both domestic and foreign firms and in Moscow and St. Petersburg many businesses specialized in filling these needs. These private security firms consisted largely of former Red Army soldiers, unemployed due to the sharp reduction in military spending, but among them were also members of clans affiliated with the Organizatsya. Such firms were not only

*Above left:
Expansion
to the East.
The commercial
freedom in the
countries of the
former Soviet Union
has fostered the
development of
legal activities like
casinos, which
are now subject
to pressure from
organized crime.*

*Following double
page: Ancient
opium dens.
This custom, once
the retreat of the
highest levels
of the Chinese
social hierarchy,
became popular
throughout
the country from
the seventeenth
century. Two
centuries later,
it spread to the
West through
the network
of Chinatowns
springing up across
the world.*

financially profitable: these seemingly legal security firms provided the perfect justification for the Mafia's possession of weapons. And, as ever, thanks to corrupt officials, organized crime was able to carry on its illegal activities almost undisturbed.

Speculation Spreads to the Balkans

The Russian Mafia also has its hierarchy; above the unskilled criminal labor there is a level that manages the connections to the political and financial speculation carried out in the Balkan countries. This new Russian oligarchy was at the center of the murky business relationships surrounding the privatization process set in motion by the Romanian government after the fall of the dictator Ceausescu. Naturalized American citizens born in Russia diverted capital obtained from aluminum and oil concessions in the former Soviet Union to this new market. The aim was to open up additional opportunities for the control of raw materials and energy, but the Romanian judiciary, suspicious of the combination of collusion and pressure on local public officials, opened inquiries and brought about charges of corruption.

The Organizatsya's interests extended to other nations in the region as well. Montenegro's Milo Djukanovic was subject to the glare of the international press because of his involvement in the sale of the largest metallurgy company in Montenegro to a Russian business owned by a controversial representative of the former Soviet oligarchy.[4]

Former Soviet republics have their own organizations, such as the Obscina, in Chechnya, whose name literally means "community." The clan, which according to some investigative sources is involved in illegal activities such as money laundering, human trafficking, drug trafficking in Central Asia, the Caucasus, and Russia, and the clandestine shipment of radioactive substances such as plutonium, got its start in the independence and liberation movements that had emerged in the 1970s against the centralized power of Moscow. This overlap of criminal and nationalist interests raises questions about the organization's true identity, in that it seemed to have used illegal activities to finance the separatist Chechen fighters, at the same time as extending its own interests in Eastern Europe for purposes of illegal trades such as tobacco smuggling.

The Opium Dens of Chinatown

Historically, the flow of Chinese migration has led to the establishment of Chinatowns in cities around the world. With the establishment of these densely populated enclaves of Chinese culture came the spread of opium use. For centuries, opium had been used to prepare sweets for holidays and festivals, but it was only in the seventeenth century that the use of pure opium as a base material for smoking began to spread widely in China. Previously, it had been the custom to mix tobacco with the by-product of the poppy flower, but following an imperial prohibition on the use of tobacco, the

population was persuaded to smoke opium in its natural state. The increase in consumption led to the import of additional quantities from India through the British East India Company. The fight between the local Chinese authorities, which were resolute in their desire to reduce the interference of the new commercial phenomenon, and of the British Empire, set off the Opium Wars between China and England in 1839 and 1856.

Then Heroin Arrived on the Market

In the nineteenth century the consumption of opium began to intersect with that of morphine, a by-product of opium capable of inducing a state of torpor similar to that experienced during dreams. There followed a further chemical manipulation of its properties, creating a substance whose use would make the fortune of generations of criminals. In 1874, while the municipal authorities in San Francisco were considering limiting the use of pure opium in the local Chinatown, an English scientist named C. R. Wright succeeded for the first time in synthesizing heroin (chemical name: diacetylmorphine) by boiling morphine on the stove. The process was perfected for the German pharmaceutical company Bayer in 1897 by Felix Hoffman, who was trying to create an effective treatment for tuberculosis, coughs, and respiratory illnesses in general. This was the official birth of heroin (from the German word *heroisch*, meaning "heroic"), which was received with enthusiasm by the international scientific community, particularly as it was believed the

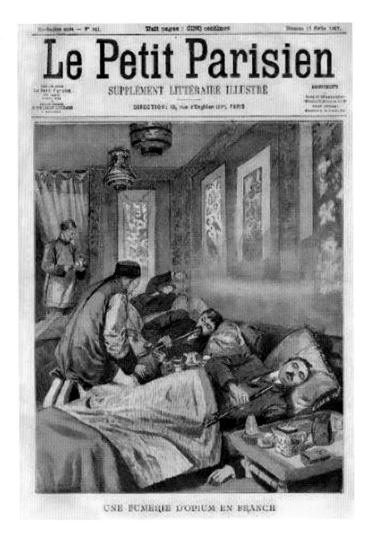

UNE FUMERIE D'OPIUM EN FRANCE

An opium den as depicted in the French popular press.

new substance would be free of the addictive qualities of its predecessor, morphine. They were spectacularly mistaken. Although its hypnotic effects are inferior to those of morphine, it is highly addictive and because of this, "recreational" use of the preparation soon became a genuine health emergency.

By 1905 it was estimated that in New York City alone some 2 tons of heroin were being consumed each year. In 1924 the Heroin Act would prohibit its production, import, and use, even for medical reasons, in the United States. This was swiftly followed by measures taken in Europe to halt the commercialization of opium, which produced mountains of white powder intended for criminal exploitation. Starting in the 1950s the new business grew to colossal proportions for the Sicilian-American Mafia. This grew further in the 1960s, and, thanks to the involvement of the United States in the Vietnam War and the willingness of American commanders to tolerate its use by soldiers (charter flights were actually organized for the transport of raw opium from Burma and Laos), the Mafia threw itself into its distribution.

In the first phase the Cosa Nostra synthesized opium from Turkey mostly in laboratories operated by criminal organizations in Marseille. After the dismantling of the so-called French Connection, a new secret channel opened, originating in the countries of the Golden Triangle*, a region of Southeast Asia that included parts of Burma, Laos, and Thailand. It was a genuine "state within a state" that specialized in the trafficking and production of drugs and that would maintain, unopposed, with the participation of Vietnam, Cambodia, and southern China, the leadership in the worldwide production of opium up until the end of the 1990s (even with cultivation in the so-called Golden Crescent of Afghanistan, Iran, and Pakistan). By this time, the countries of the Golden Triangle had acquired the chemical know-how to refine heroin themselves and to place it in the distribution network, without relying on the less profitable export of pure product.

The Chinese Triad

Drug trafficking, money laundering, gambling, prostitution, and auto theft, as well as counterfeit computer programs and contraband music CDs and films: thanks to new technologies allowing copying on an industrial scale, these activities have made organized crime a powerful part of the global economy. The same goes for the Chinese Triad*, a criminal organization with supposed roots in the efforts of a Masonic-style society established in China in the mid-eighteenth century called Tian di Hui ("Society of Heaven and Earth") to overthrow the Qing dynasty and restore the Ming dynasty. Today the Triad has its base of operations in Hong Kong but also is active in Taiwan, Macau, and the various Chinatowns in North America, Europe, South Africa, Australia, and New Zealand. In Hong Kong, where the Triad has its headquarters, there are about sixty active affiliated clans that oversee the management of petty street crime. The brains of the organization make use of a plethora of abbreviations (such as 14K, Wo Shing Wo, and Sun Yee On) that have extended their relationships to the highest levels of worldwide organized crime.

The Business of Cocaine and the South American Mafias

The Medellin cartel* of Colombia, a large organization of drug traffickers active in the international cocaine trade in the 1970s and 1980s, now seems like a distant memory, at least compared to the "brokers" of the white powder that today is snorted in industrial quantities by the upper-middle classes in the West. The cartel was later defeated through the intelligence work of the U.S. Drug Enforcement Agency (DEA), established in 1973 by Richard Nixon, in order to consolidate all anti-drug efforts within the

Department of Justice. Prior its defeat, the Medellin cartel split the cocaine market with another Colombian organization, the Cali cartel. The group in Cali put itself in direct competition with its rivals in Medellin, in a battle that saw the two groups fight to the sound of gunfire for supremacy over the territory.

In 2000 the management of the finished product, as well as its geography, changed its points of reference. The globalization of the economy and the increase in cocaine consumption (estimated to be used by 250 million people worldwide), pushed all criminal organizations to modify the entire system of profits related to their illegal activities in South America. The gangs sheltered themselves from the risks connected to the purchase, shipment, and sale of cocaine by using new middlemen and employing techniques borrowed from the world of high finance. They now used intermediaries at every stage, from dealing with the drug lords, to production and final delivery overseas. These drug businesses established front companies or made use of seemingly legitimate businesses to oversee administrative issues such as the customs clearance of the cargo concealing the product.[5] Investigations carried out in Europe would identify the creation of a true multinational criminal entity that was engaged in drug trafficking. It was represented by the Colombian, Peruvian, and other South American cartels for production, and the Mafia groups in the consumer countries for financing. Around the main office that managed the entire flow there revolved a myriad of import-export businesses and transport companies (both sea and land) that

were perfectly legal and that guaranteed, through banking channels, finance companies, and the use of the Internet, the success of operations intended to produce a return on investment equal to 300 percent of the initial cost of the prohibited substances. It was a multiplier that no legal industrial or financial activity could ever guarantee, which explains in part why the new organizations that today manage the traffic in drugs on an international scale prefer to fight their battles with the computer mouse rather than gunfire.[6]

This formidable network had emerged from the hidden connections between the Calabrian 'Ndrangheta and the Mafia groups present in Mexico. In December 2009, in a gun battle in the city of Cuernavaca, Mexican police killed Arturo Beltrán Leyva, considered the "boss of bosses" of the Federación*. This group had successfully infiltrated the stronghold of the cartels that, at least up until 2008, had shared out the business of transporting and distributing drugs. Despite the death of Beltrán Leyva, investigators are now convinced that the new bosses in the global market for white powder are to be sought in Mexico and Italy.[7]

Other Criminal Organizations Look to the Sea

There are other organizations present on the international crime scene. Their countries of origin may have less economic clout, but they are no less dangerous from the point of view of criminal activity. Among these is Turkey, the longtime base of operations of Alaatin

Cakici, a mafioso believed to belong to the ultranationalist group known as the Gray Wolves and who is part of the organization that manages various illegal activities in his country. Extradited from France in 2008 but released by the Turkish courts, he was later arrested in Austria and then sentenced for various crimes committed in 2004 in Turkey, where he received a sentence in the Tekirdag maximum security prison. In Albania, meanwhile, the mafia has turned illegal immigration into a real business. For a price, Albanian mafiosi will arrange passage to the Italian coast from the Balkans. Their customers, all Albanians, are so desperate to cross the Adriatic they are willing to travel in overburdened inflatable dinghies, constantly exposed to the danger of stormy seas and shipwreck.

Anti-Mafia extraditions. Alaattin Cakici in court in Istanbul on July 13, 2004. Arrested by the Austrian police in October during one of his extraordinary trips across Europe, the boss was sent back to Turkey. The Vienna Court of Appeal rejected the defense's appeal: In his country, the judges said, Cakici will undergo a fair trial and will not risk being tortured or killed in prison.

Left: People trafficking. Mass disembarkation of immigrants from the Balkans on the Italian coast. This business, run by Albanian clans, is at the center of frantic activity, generating great sums of money despite the controls and patrols of the authorities.

Below: Centers for identification and expulsion. Repatriation procedures for illegal immigrants arriving in Italy often end up shipwrecked in a sea of bureaucracy. The authorities are frequently hampered by the rules for immigration set by the European Union.

THE **MAFIA** AND **FILM**

The Mafia in the movies, from the first depictions
of Al Capone to Marlon Brando in the film saga
The Godfather to the amateur actors in the film Gomorra,
a recent portrayal of the new Neapolitan Camorra.

Scarface. *Al Pacino as Tony Montana, in a scene from the film*
written by Oliver Stone and directed by Brian De Palma.

The First Shots of the 1930s

The relationship between cinema and the world of organized crime first began in the 1930s. Before its appearance on the silver screen the Mafia as a phenomenon was not known by the general public as extensively as it is today. Cinema changed that, and contributed to spreading the myth of the Mafia. Today, the world of vendettas, *omertà,* and criminal family connections are familiar far beyond the reaches of Italian communities, a fact largely due to their depiction in the cinema. The now-clichéd image of the gangster with his tommy gun concealed in a violin case dates from the films produced during the 1930s.

In the earliest group of films dedicated to the criminal underworld, a prominent place is reserved for *Little Caesar,* directed by Mervyn LeRoy in 1930 and adapted from the novel by W. R. Burnett. The plot tells the story of Caesar Enrico Bandello (played by Edward G. Robinson), an ambitious criminal who leaves the countryside for a life of crime in the big city. Robinson's performance as "Rico" set the template for Hollywood depictions of gangsters for decades to come. The film itself became a recognized part of the pantheon of cinema when, in 2000, it was chosen by the National Film Registry of the Library of Congress for restoration and conservation for the benefit of future generations.

The Power of *Omertà*: *In the Name of the Law* and *The Day of the Owl*

In the Name of the Law ("In Nome della Legge" in Italian) was one of the first Italian-French productions to depict the world of the Sicilian Mafia with extreme realism. Its evocation of the enormous power of *omertà* in protecting the gangs from inquiries into their illegal activities is particularly effective. Directed by the Italian Pietro Germi, and based on the novel *Piccola Pretura* by Giuseppe Guido Lo Schiavo, a judge, the film tells the story of a magistrate in Palermo, Guido Schiavi (played by Massimo Girotti), who is sent to a small town in the hinterlands of Sicily in the late 1940s to combat the increasing social injustice in an area controlled by the local boss, Turi Passalacqua (played by Charles Vanel). Schiavi's battle against the wall of complicity that protects the local clan is fought completely alone, but at the end it enables him to establish the law and order in an environment tenaciously accustomed to resisting any type of change imposed from outside.

Another accurate depiction of the traits and behavior of the Mafia is seen in the 1968 Italian-French co-production *The Day of the Owl* ("Il giorno della civetta"). Directed by Damiano Damiani and based on a the novel of the same name by Leonardo Sciascia, a member of the Sicilian parliament who wrote extensively about the Mafia, the film follows the inquiry by Captain Bellodi (played by Franco Nero), an officer in the carabinieri sent from northern Italy to a small town in rural Sicily. Bellodi investigates the murder of a building contractor who, as he will

learn, was killed by a shotgun blast for refusing to give a contract to a company protected by the local bosses. The film, like the novel, creates a vivid portrait of a rural Mafia ready to make the leap to the higher levels of organized crime; a world full of compromises and corruption in which the interests of obliging officials are intertwined with those of the bosses who control the territory. The plot is enriched by other figures who live on the border between the legal world and the illegal underworld and who are part of the real-life background of the Mafia. One of these is the police informant Parrineddu (played by Serge Reggiani), who gives his information to Captain Bellodi one piece at a time, under the eye of the local godfathers who are perfectly aware of his role as a paid informer. It is a modus vivendi that, within certain limits, is tolerated by the Mafia simply because Parrineddu must still earn a living, even if his job is to be a snitch. At bottom, his confessions are harmless, because they can easily be countered by "friends of friends*" when dealing with any resulting legal proceedings. Ultimately, the film proves that, despite Bellodi's best efforts, this tangled and extensive web of the criminal underworld and the official "upper world," thwart all his attempts at delivering justice.

Depictions of Salvatore Giuliano, the Bandit of Montelepre

There are two films dedicated to Salvatore Giuliano, the bandit of Montelepre, who ordered the massacre of Portella della Ginestra in 1947,

when men under his command fired on a gathering of peasants who had come to celebrate May Day. The first is an Italian production, *Salvatore Giuliano*, directed by Francesco Rosi in 1961. It is about an investigation into many of the unanswered questions behind the event. Faithful to the realism that characterizes his other work, Rosi used Sicilian dialect and reconstructed the events surrounding the discovery of Giuliano's body in the town of Castelvetrano. His film explores the contradictions in the official version put forth by the authorities, which claimed the bandit's death was the result of a gun battle with the police. The film continues with a narration of the events that followed his death and the conclusion of the trial that in 1951 sentenced some of his men to life in prison. It also tells the fate of his lieutenant, Gaspare Pisciotta, who was poisoned in prison in 1954 by coffee laced with strychnine.

In 1987 Michael Cimino revisted the story in *The Sicilian*. It was adapted from the novel of the same name by Mario Puzo. The film is in the form of an autobiography of Giuliano (played by Christopher Lambert), who is portrayed as an outlaw and firm supporter of Sicilian independence and of Sicily's annexation by the United States. The film lingers over events in the criminal life of Giuliano, who is seen as part separatist outlaw and part avenger of the poor in the manner of Robin Hood, his crimes done in the name of liberating the poorest social classes. The film is controversial for many historians in that it presents as fact certain developments that

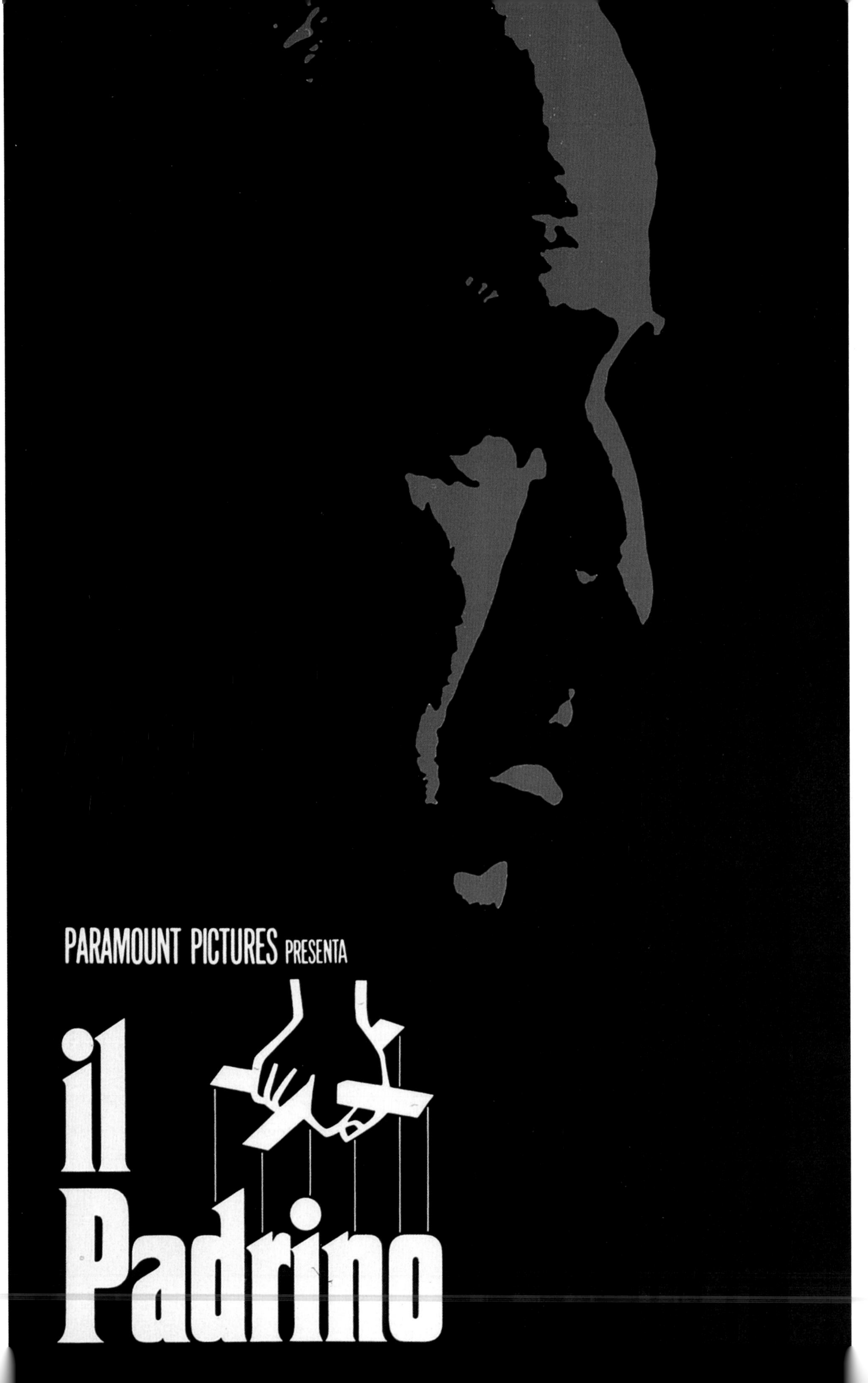
PARAMOUNT PICTURES PRESENTA
il
Padrino

are known only to be conjecture. The depiction of the massacre of Portella della Ginestra only touches on the murky areas that still surround the actual unfolding of events, one of which is the suggestion, based on a memoir by Guiliano himself, that the massacre was the result of an accident in which the men under his command fired into the crowd rather than over their heads as had been originally planned. In this film, blame was unambiguously diverted away from Giuliano to his lieutenant, thus leaving his reputation as hero/outlaw intact.

The Godfather trilogy

With the release of the film *The Godfather* in 1972, the notoriety of the Sicilian-American Mafia and its place of origin, Corleone, Sicily, spread even further across the globe. Based on the novel of the same name by Mario Puzo, an American writer of Italian origin, and directed by Francis Ford Coppola, the film was the first in a series of three, followed by *The Godfather: Part II* in 1974 and *The Godfather: Part III* in 1990. These films made up a saga that has become part of cinematic history. Marlon Brando's performance as Don Vito Corleone, a Sicilian immigrant who came to the United States in the early 1900s and became one of the most powerful Mafia bosses in New York, would, along with an exceptional cast that included Al Pacino and James Caan, help the film win three Oscars in 1973, for Best Picture, Best Actor in a Leading Role, and Best Screenplay Adaptation.

The film depicts all the elements linking Sicily and the United States in the real-life history of organized crime; because of this, the film attracted controversy even before it started shooting. The Italian American Civil Rights League, led by the Mafia don Joseph Colombo, argued that the as-of-yet unmade film was offensive to Italian Americans, and staged a protest in New York's Madison Square Gardens in an attempt to stop it being made. Continued pressure was put on the film's producers to cease production, including– so it is alleged–threats of violence. Eventually an agreement was reached: filming could continue as long as the word "mafia" never appeared in the movie.

But there was no need to use the word directly: the explicit and nuanced depiction of an Italian organized crime family speaks volumes. Brando's performance is the embodiment of a certain personality created by a particular culture and way of life. Even his physical appearance attests to the life of the character: his heavy cheeks (courtesy of a dental apparatus kept today in the American Museum of the Moving Image in Queens) gives Brando the worn-out look of an experienced, powerful Mafia boss. According to some, he resembled the real-life godfather Carlo Gambino, who ascended to the upper reaches of the American Cosa Nostra. He was reserved and standoffish, careful to avoid any notoriety in the newspapers. Gambino, and the film character that resembled him, represented the "old Mafia."

Other characters in the film also drew inspiration from real-life mafiosi. Don Vito's *consigliere*, Tom Hagen (played by Robert Duvall), seemed modeled on the position that Lucky Luciano sought to establish in each of the families.

At the heart of Coppola's saga: The entire evolution of the Cosa Nostra phenomenon, from the traditional mafia family run by Don Vito Corleone (Marlon Brando) in The Godfather to the more modern and ruthless version run by his "heir", Michael Corleone (Al Pacino) in The Godfather: Part II. The Godfather: Part III, with Andy Garcia (as Vincent Mancini) is dedicated to the links between the Mafia, politics and the Vatican banks.

The *consigliere* played a peacekeeping role, and was fulfilled by the person most temperamentally suited to calming the previously very violent relationships between the Cosa Nostra families.

Plot developments from the film also echo recent Mafia history. Don Vito urges his son Michael (played by Al Pacino) to return to Sicily in order to escape the ferocious fallout from a bloody chain of vendettas. In real life other Sicilian immigrants to the United States made the return journey for the same reason. Later in the film, when Michael takes on his father's mantel as the head of the family, he punishes rival families for various betrayals in the measured and calculated manner of the real-life Cosa Nostra. All three films employ sufficient parallels and echoes with the activities of real-life crime figures and the recent history of the American Cosa Nostra to avoid the need to mention the word "mafia" at all.

Al Capone and *The Untouchables,* in television and film

The gangsterism of the 1930s is the subject of the 1987 film *The Untouchables,* directed by Brian De Palma. It won an Oscar in 1988 for Best Supporting Actor, for Sean Connery in the role of Jimmy Malone, an incorruptible policeman of Irish background. The screenplay portrays a Mafia that was more instinctive and less analytical in its decision-making than the one that appears in *The Godfather.* In De Palma's rendition, the gangs are engaged in a continuous and bloody struggle for domination of the illegal alcohol trade in Prohibition-era Chicago. The plot revolves around the attempt to put Capone

behind bars, and explores the collusion between the Mafia and greedy government officials. Like many cinematic treatments inspired by the actual history of the Mafia, the film plays with elements of realism and fiction: the initial scene in the barber shop, for example, was shot using original furnishings from the establishment used by the real Capone. Other elements were fabricated for the purposes of story telling; for example, despite his death in the film, Frank Nitti survived to become the leader of Capone's organization. *The Untouchables* is also the title of a TV series that appeared on the American network ABC between 1959 and 1963. The series, created by the producer Quinn Martin and set between 1929 and 1935, very probably inspired De Palma and tells, using a lot of license with respect to Prohibition-era events, the story of the police squad led by Eliot Ness who caught the gangster of Chicago. The central thread running through this and the Sean Connery film is the extreme violence in every episode, which at the time was the subject of various protests but also of a noteworthy public success. The remake of *The Untouchables,* shown in the USA between January 1993 and May 1994, did not have such success. The constant superimposition of fiction and reality also returned, in many ways, in the more famous, recent series *The Sopranos.* In fact, the extreme realism of some scenes and the sheer

Robert de Niro plays the famous mafioso Al Capone in Brian De Palma's The Untouchables.

The Sopranos, mafia and television. At the centre, James Gandolfini as Tony Soprano, the boss of the Italian-American family and the protagonist in the well-known television series broadcast by HBO until 2007.

rawness of the language represented one of the highly successful elements of the series created by David Chase and produced by the American network HBO between 1999 and 2007. The series, which thrilled the general public in the United States and elsewhere, tells the story of a New Jersey immigrant family originally from Avellino, in Campania. The paterfamilias, Tony Soprano, is the archetype as well as the stereotype of the typical Italian-American boss: a character who borrows traits and ways of behaving from the five mafia families who really shared power in New York's criminal underworld. The series, with numerous actors of Italian origin, has picked up all the most important TV awards (among them five Golden Globes and three Emmys), but also heavy criticism since it has been accused of bringing the Italian communities of the United States into disrepute.

Scarface and the Gilded World of Cocaine

The 1983 film *Scarface*, also directed by Brian De Palma, with a screenplay by Oliver Stone, depicts the more recent activities of organized crime in the illegal distribution of cocaine. It is a remake of the 1930s film of the same name by Howard Hawks, which revolves around the figure of Al Capone, but replaces Prohibition-era Chicago with the 1980s Miami drug trade. In De

Palma's *Scarface*, the underworld is represented by an immigrant Cuban community engaged in various illegal activities.

It also plays with historical fact to create a fictional story with parallels with reality: in the film Tony Montana, nicknamed Scarface (played by Al Pacino) is among the more than one hundred and twenty-five thousand refugees allowed to leave Cuba in 1980, with the undeclared purpose of emptying out the prisons of Havana. Soon after his arrival, he and his friend Manny Ribera (played by Steven Bauer) quit their badly paid jobs and become links in chain of cocaine distribution. In the film, the methods of control used by the bosses are inspired by actual events, such as the scene in which a member of Montana's gang is killed with a chain saw. In writing his script, Stone consulted, among others, the Miami police and the Drug Enforcement Administration of the U.S. Department of Justice.

The film's reflections on the activities of organized crime in Miami aroused protests from the city's Cuban community, which accused the producers of discrediting recent immigrants by portraying them as criminals, and of ignoring the fact that many of the exiles had suffered repression in Cuba because of their anti-Castro activities. The refusal by the producers to change the plot forced them to shoot in Los Angeles some of the exterior shots that had been planned for Miami.

The Neapolitan Camorra

Events in the history of the Mafia and of other criminal organizations from southern Italy, such as the Neapolitan Camorra, figure prominently in various Italian artistic works. These take their cue from individual episodes, or from the life stories of important figures in the fight against organized crime, often going into the details of the bloodiest events. *Il camorrista*, a 1986 debut film by the director Giuseppe Tornatore, entered the Neapolitan underworld through a loose adaptation of the novel of the same name by Giuseppe Marrazzo. The main character in that fictional world is the Professor of Vesuvius (in Neapolitan dialect "O professore 'e vesuviano"). Through this imaginary character (played by Ben Gazzara), Tornatore depicts events and crimes that can be connected to the real-life Neapolitan boss, Raffaele Cutolo, the founder of the New Camorra that dominated Naples starting in the 1970s.

The 2008 film *Gomorra* is set in the Neapolitan neighborhood of Le Vele di Scampia ("The Sails of Scampia"), which is pervaded by drug trafficking and unemployment. It is based on the best-seller of the same name by Roberto Saviano, a young Italian writer who describes the world of the Neapolitan Camorra after having lived in close contact with its members. This film, which won the Special Grand Jury Prize in Cannes that same year, depicts the violent and savage criminal underworld of Campania with crude realism. Some of the actors are amateurs who come from that same world where murder, blackmail, and extortion are everyday events. Some of those who appear in the film were real-life criminals who ended up in handcuffs not long after the film was first screened.

The main difference between the narrative of this film and other works about organized crime is, above all, that it depicts the reality of the bosses as it truly is, from the point of view of someone who lives it and suffers it. "Michael Corleone [is] beautiful," writes Saviano, because "he is a man who is tormented, fascinating, and powerful, but who has his own rules. You have contempt for him, but you identify with him. In *Gomorra*, this could not be allowed to happen. You had to be right next to the stench of the poisoned fish that had been smuggled ashore; you had to feel the misery of someone waiting for a Camorrista's monthly wage."[1] In other words, *Gomorra* appears to have achieved one of the goals wished for in 1965 by a judge such as Cesare Terranova, who paid with his life for investigations into the Sicilian Mafia: "putting to one side the fantasies of the past," said Terranova, one must understand that "the Mafia is not an abstract concept, it is not a state of mind, but organized crime, efficient and dangerous. . . . There exists but one Mafia; not old, not young, not good, not bad; a criminal association." Saviano's book and the film of the same name is the first step in putting aside the mythologies to address the reality.

Above: A writer penetrates the Mafia. Roberto Saviano on a TV program in Italy. His true story about the Neapolitan Camorra is the product of a genuine infiltration of the world of organized crime. The success of Gomorra has meant that the author has to live under constant police protection.

Facing page: Bulletproof. A scene from the film based on Roberto Saviano's book. The act of defiance of two guaglioni (boys, in local dialect), who wanted to compete with the Camorra bosses, leads them to a trap and ultimately to their execution on a beach.

FILMOGRAPHY

Little Caesar, 1931, directed by Mervyn LeRoy

The Public Enemy, 1931, directed by William A. Wellman

Scarface, 1932, directed by Howard Hawks

In the Name of the Law (*In nome della legge*), 1949, directed by Pietro Germi

The Magistrate (*Il magistrato*), 1960, directed by Luigi Zampa [*The Honored Society*], (*L'onorata società*), 1961, directed by Riccardo Pazzaglia

Salvatore Giuliano (id.), 1962, directed by Francesco Rosi

Mafioso (id.), 1962, directed by Alberto Lattuada

Hands Over the City (*Le mani sulla città*), 1963, directed by Francesco Rosi

Two Gangsters in the Wild West (*Due mafiosi nel Far West*), 1964, directed by Giorgio Simonelli

We Still Kill the Old Way (*A ciascuno il suo*), 1967, directed by Elio Petri

The Day of the Owl (*Il giorno della civetta*), 1968, directed by Damiano Damiani

The Godfather, 1972, directed by Francis Ford Coppola

The Mattei Affair (*Il caso Mattei*), 1972, directed by Francesco Rosi

The Valachi Papers, 1972, directed by Terence Young

Gang War in Naples (*Camorra*), 1972, directed by Pasquale Squitieri

Lucky Luciano (id.), 1973, directed by Francesco Rosi

Wipeout! (*Il boss*), 1973, directed by Fernando Di Leo

The Godfather: Part II, 1974, directed by Francis Ford Coppola

The Yakuza, 1974, directed by Sydney Pollack

The Killing of a Chinese Bookie, 1976, directed by John Cassavetes

The Iron Prefect (*Il prefetto di ferro*), 1977, directed by Pasquale Squitieri

Father of the Godfathers (*Corleone*), 1981, directed by Pasquale Squitieri

Scarface, 1983, directed by Brian De Palma

Picone Sent Me (*Mi manda Picone*), 1984, directed by Nanni Loy

Once Upon a Time in America, 1984, directed by Sergio Leone

[*One Hundred Days in Palermo*], (*Cento giorni a Palermo*), 1984, directed by Giuseppe Ferrara

The Sicilian Connection (*Pizza Connection*), 1985, directed by Damiano Damiani

Prizzi's Honor, 1985, directed by John Huston

The Repenter (*Il pentito*), 1985, directed by Pasquale Squitieri

The Professor (*Il camorrista*), 1986, directed by Giuseppe Tornatore

The Untouchables, 1987, directed by Brian De Palma

The Sicilian, 1987, directed by Michael Cimino

[*The Prize at Stake*], (*La posta in gioco*), 1988, directed by Sergio Nasca

Black Rain, 1989, directed by Ridley Scott

Forever Mary (*Mery per sempre*), 1989, directed by Marco Risi

The Godfather: Part III, 1990, directed by Francis Ford Coppola

King of New York, 1990, directed by Abel Ferrara

The Palermo Connection (*Dimenticare Palermo*), 1990, directed by Francesco Rosi

Goodfellas, 1990, directed by Martin Scorsese

Billy Bathgate, 1991, directed by Robert Benton

Johnny Stecchino (id.), 1991, directed by Roberto Benigni

Mobsters, 1991, directed by Michael Karbelnikoff

Minbo—or the Gentle Art of Japanese Extortion (*Minbo no onna*), 1992, directed by J z Itami

The Escort (*La scorta*), 1993, directed by Ricky Tognazzi

Giovanni Falcone (id.), 1993, directed by Giuseppe Ferrara

A Bronx Tale, 1993, directed by Robert De Niro

Carlito's Way, 1993, directed by Brian De Palma

The Long Silence (*Il lungo silenzio*), 1993, directed by Margarethe Von Trotta

Ordinary Hero (*Un eroe borghese*), 1995, directed by Michele Placido

Paolo Borsellino (id.), 1995, directed by Pasquale Scimeca

Casino, 1995, directed by Martin Scorsese

The Uncle from Brooklyn (*Lo zio di Brooklyn*), 1995, directedby Daniele Ciprì and Franco Maresco

Palermo-Milan One Way (*Palermo Milano solo andata*), 1996, directed by Claudio Fragasso

Strangled lives (*Vite strozzate*), 1996, directed by Ricky Tognazzi

An Eyewitness Account (*Testimone a rischio*), 1996, directed by Pasquale Pozzessere

To Die for Tano (*Tano da morire*), 1997, directed by Roberta Torre

Donnie Brasco, 1997, directed by Mike Newell

Rehearsal for War (*Teatro di guerra*), 1998, directed by Mario Martone

Excellent Cadavers, 1999, directed by Ricky Tognazzi

The Sopranos, 1999-2007, TV series directed by Jack Bender

Lansky, 1999, directed by John McNaughton

Analyze This, 1999, directed by Harold Ramis

Brother, 2000, directed by Takeshi Kitano

Placido Rizzotto (id.), 2000, directed by Pasquale Scimeca

One Hundred Steps (*I cento passi*), 2000, directed by Marco Tullio Giordana

Traffic, 2000, directed by Steven Soderbergh

Red Moon (*Luna rossa*), 2001, directed by Antonio Capuano

Angela (id.), 2002, directed by Roberta Torre

Road to Perdition, 2002, directed by Sam Mendes

Analyze That, 2002, directed by Harold Ramis

My Brother-In-Law (*Mio cognato*), 2003, directed by Alessandro Piva

Secret file (*Segreti di stato*), 2003, directed by Paolo Benvenuti

I'm Not Scared (*Io non ho paura*), 2003, directed by Gabriele Salvatores

A Children's Story (*Certi bambini*), 2004, directed by Andrea and Antonio Frazzi

Paolo Borsellino (id.), 2004, TV miniseries directed by Gianluca Maria Tavarelli

In the Light of the Sun (*Alla luce del sole*), 2005, directed by Roberto Faenza

The Mafia is White (*La mafia è bianca*), 2005, directed by Stefano Maria Bianchi and Alberto Nerazzini

Excellent Cadavers (*In un altro paese*), 2005, directed by Marco Turco

Crime Novel (*Romanzo criminale*), 2005, directed by Michele Placido

Joe Petrosino (id.), 2006, TV series directed by Alfredo Peyretti

[*The Ghost of Corleone*], (*Il fantasma di Corleone*), 2006, directed by Marco Amenta

Find Me Guilty, 2006, directed by Sidney Lumet

The Departed, 2006, directed by Martin Scorsese

Man of Glass (*L'uomo di vetro*), 2007, directed Stefano Incerti

[*Milan-Palermo the Return*], (*Milano-Palermo: il ritorno*), 2007, directed by Claudio Fragasso

The Sweet and the Bitter (*Il dolce e l'amaro*), 2007, directed by Andrea Porporati

Eastern Promises, 2007, directed by David Cronenberg

Gomorrah (*Gomorra*), 2008, directed by Matteo Garrone

Il Divo (*Il divo*), 2008, directed by Paolo Sorrentino

Public Enemies, 2009, directed by Michael Mann

Fortapàsc (id.), 2009, directed by Marco Risi

NOTES

The Origins of the Mafia

1. Saverio Lodato, *Trent'anni di mafia* (Milan: Rizzoli, 2006), 487 ff.
2. Leone Zingales, *Il Padrino ultimo atto* (Reggio Emilia: Alberti editore, 2006), photo appendix, 8.
3. Leonardo Sciascia, *Cruciverba* (Milan: Adelphi, 1998), 171.
4. Henner Hess, *Mafia* (Roma-Bari: Laterza, 1993), 192.
5. See, among others, Felice Cavallaro, *Mafia album di Cosa Nostra* (Milan: Rizzoli, 1992), 3 and Salvatore Lupo, *History of the Mafia* (New York: Columbia University Press, 2009), 50.
6. Salvatore Francesco Romano, *Breve storia della Sicilia* (Turin: Edizioni Rai, Radiotelevisione Italiana, 1964), 187.
7. On this point see Cavallaro, 3.
8. In the Historical Archive of the Museo Nazionale in Naples, Fondo Nisco, 15, XLVIII-LIV.
9. Leopoldo Franchetti, "Condizioni politiche e amministrative della Sicilia," in *La Sicilia nel 1876* (L. Franchetti and S. Sonnino, Eulogos, 2007), edition Intra Text (www.intratext.com/IXT/ITA2434/_P1K.htm) taken from the edition printed by Vallecchi, Florence, 1925, Book One, chapter I, paragraph 27.
10. Ibid.
11. Michele Pantaleone, *The Mafia and Politics* (New York: Coward-McCann, 1966), 8.
12. Franchetti, Book One, chapter I, paragraph 38.
13. Pantaleone, 10–15.
14. Lupo, 66.
15. Ibid., 52.
16. John Dickie, *Cosa Nostra, A History of the Sicilian Mafia* (New York: St. Martin's Press, 2004), 51 and 53.
17. Lupo, 50–51.
18. Giuseppe Carlo Marino, *Storia della mafia* (Rome: Newton Compton editori, 1998), 62–63.
19. Lupo, 81 and 94.
20. Franchetti, Book One, chapter II, paragraph 30.
21. Marino, 62–63.
22. Lupo, 72.
23. Sidney Sonnino, "I contadini in Sicilia," in *La Sicilia nel 1876* (L. Franchetti and S. Sonnino, Eulogos, 2007), edition Intra Text (www.intratext.com/IXT/ITA2434/_P1K.htm) taken from the edition printed by Vallecchi, Florence, 1925, Book Two, supplementary chapter, paragraph 133.
24. Marino, 81 ff.
25. See among others, Tommaso Pedio, *Inchiesta Massari sul brigantaggio* (Manduria-Bari-Rome: Pietro Lacaita Editore, 1998); Antonio Mattei, *Brigantaggio sommerso* (Rome: Scipioni editori, 1980); AA.VV "Sisto V e il brigantaggio nello Stato pontificio" in *Roma e i suoi personaggi* (Rome: Pubblicità Progresso, 1967); Alfio Cavoli, *Lo sparviere della Maremma* (Rome: Scipioni editori, 1990); José Borgès, *La mia vita tra i briganti* (Manduria-Bari-Rome: Pietro Lacaita Editore, 1964); Giovanni Conti, *L'Italia nella servitù* (Rome: Casa editrice italiana, 1952); Gaetano Cingari, *Brigantaggio, proprietari e contadini nel Sud (1799-1900)* (Reggio Calabria: Editori meridionali riuniti, 1976).
26. Lupo, 51.
27. Ernesto Pontieri, *Il riformismo borbonico nella Sicilia del '700 e dell'800* (Naples: Edizioni Scientifiche Italiane, 1965), 243.
28. Vittorio Paliotti, *Storia della Camorra* (Rome: Newton Compton editori, 2006), 77 ff.
29. Ibid., 199 ff.

The Mafia in the United States

1. Salvatore Lupo, *History of the Mafia* (New York: Columbia University Press, 2009), 177.
2. See Giuseppe Carlo Marino, *Storia della mafia* (Rome: Newton Compton editori, 1998), 101.
3. Selwyn Raab, *Le famiglie di Cosa Nostra* (Rome: Newton Compton editori, 2009), 31.
4. Salvatore Lupo, *Quando la mafia trovò l'America* (Turin: Einaudi, 2008), 23.
5. Lupo, *History of the Mafia*, 180.
5. Lupo, *Quando la mafia trovò l'America*, 36.
7. Ibid., 16.
8. Arrigo Petacco, *Joe Petrosino* (New York: Macmillan, 1974), 31.
9. Ibid., 34 ff.
10. Leonardo Sciascia, "La storia della mafia," in *Storia illustrata*, (April 1972): 47.
11. Gaetano Falzone, *Storia della mafia* (Milan: Pan editrice, 1975), 195.
12. Gianluca Tenti, *Mafia americana* (Florence: Editoriale Olimpia, 2006), 43.
13. Andre Valmont, *Gangsters contro G-men* (Geneva: Editions de Crémille, 1968), 17.
14. Lupo, *Quando la mafia trovò l'America*, 49.
15. Tenti, 71.
16. Valmont, 48.
17. Lupo, *Quando la mafia trovò l'America*, 50.
18. Raab, 51.
19. Tenti, 105 ff.
20. Sciascia, 46
21. Raab, 549.

Lucky Luciano and the Cosa Nostra get Involved in International Politics

1. Selwyn Raab, *Le famiglie di Cosa Nostra* (Rome: Newton Compton editori, 2009), 46.
2. Salvatore Lupo, *Quando la mafia trovò l'America* (Turin: Einaudi, 2008), 66.
3. Raab, 39.
4. Lupo, 110.
5. Raab, 42.
6. Lupo, 61.
7. Raab, 44.
8. Lupo, 63.
9. Ibid., 52.
10. Raab, 41 and 48.
11. Lupo, 96 ff.
12. Estes Kefauver, *Crime in America* (New York: Doubleday & Co., 1959), 33.
13. Lupo, 127.

14. Ibid., 128.
15. Gianluca Tenti, *Mafia americana* (Florence: Editoriale Olimpia, 2006), 143.
16. Lupo, 226.
17. Kefauver, 48 and 49.
18. Giuseppe Casarrubea and Mario J.Cereghino, *Lupara Nera* (Milan: Bompiani, 2009), 177 ff.
19. Ibid., 179.
20. Michele Pantaleone, *The Mafia and Politics* (New York: Coward-McCann, 1966), 46.
21. John Dickie, *Cosa Nostra, A History of the Sicilian Mafia* (New York: St. Martin's Press, 2004), 276.
22. Ibid., 277.
23. Lupo, 141.
24. Giuseppe Carlo Marino, *Storia della mafia* (Rome: Newton Compton editori, 1998), 153.
25. Dickie, 271.
26. Ibid., 268.
27. Casarrubea and Cereghino, 169.
28. Pantaleone, 44.
29. Casarrubea and Cereghino, 169.
30. Jim Garrison, *JFK, sulle tracce degli assassini* (Milan: Sperling & Kupfer, 1992), 14 and 15.
31. Dale Myers, *Secrets of a Homicide*, featured in the documentary, *Peter Jennings Reporting: The Kennedy Assassination, Beyond Conspiracy,* first aired on ABC television in November 2003.
32. Raab, 154 and 155.

The Mafia and Politics in Postwar Italy

1. Paola Baroni and Paolo Benvenuti, *Segreti di Stato* (Rome: Fandango Libri, 2003), 41.
2. Giuseppe Casarrubea and Mario J. Cereghino, *Lupara Nera* (Milan: Bompiani, 2009), 321.
3. Giuseppe Carlo Marino, *Storia della mafia*, (Rome: Newton Compton editori, 1998), 186.
4. Salvatore Lupo, *History of the Mafia* (New York: Columbia University Press, 2009), 230.
5. National Archives Records Administration, rg., 126, s. 210, b. 432, f. 8, cited in Casarrubea and Cereghino, 370.
6. Ibid., rg., 226, s. 174, b. 141, f. 1048, *Political Events*, cited in Casarrubea and Cereghino, 372.
7. A.G.D. Maran, *Mafia, Inside the Dark Heart* (London-Edinburgh: Mainstream Publishing, 2009), 150.
8. Marino, 222.
9. Ibid., 268.
10. Michele Falzone, *Mafia. Dal feudo all'eccidio di Via carini* (Palermo: Flaccovio editrice, 1983).
11. Umberto Lucentini, *Paolo Borsellino. Il valore di una vita* (Milan: San Paolo edizioni, 2006), 290.
12. See article by Lirio Abbate, "Tra mafia e Stato," *L'Espresso, 43* (October 29, 2009).

Bosses, Godfathers, and Women of the Mafia

1. Michele Pantaleone, *The Mafia and Politics* (New York: Coward-McCann, 1966), 46.
2. John Dickie, *Cosa Nostra: A History of the Sicilian Mafia* (New York: St. Martin's Press, 2004), 79.
3. Danilo Dolci, *Waste* (New York: Monthly Review Press, 1963), 61.
4. Ibid., 183.

5. Gianluca Tenti, *Mafia americana* (Florence: Editoriale Olimpia, 2006), 66.

6. Dickie, 271.

7. Dolci, 58.

8. Pantaleone, 58.

9. Dickie, 279.

10. Rosario Poma and Enzo Perrone, *La mafia, nonni e nipoti* (Florence: Vallecchi, 1971), 33 (first photo appendix).

11. Michele Pantaleone, *L'antimafia in tribunale* (Naples: Centro editoriale del Mezzogiorno (CEM), 1976), 64 (first photo appendix).

12. Nicola Tranfaglia, *Mafia politica e affari 1943-91* (Bari: Laterza, 1992), 49 ff.

13. Michele Pantaleone, *Mafia e droga* (Turin: Einaudi, 1966), 123.

14. Estes Kefauver, *Crime in America* (New York: Doubleday & Co., 1959), 38.

15. Salvatore Lupo, *Quando la mafia trovò l'America* (Turin: Einaudi, 2008), 165.

16. Selwyn Raab, *Le famiglie di Cosa Nostra* Rome: Newton Compton editori, 2009), 154 and 155.

17. Giuseppe Casarrubea and Mario J. Cereghino, *Lupara Nera* (Milan: Bompiani, 2009), 188.

18. Pantaleone, *Mafia e droga*, 78.

19. Salvatore Lupo, *History of the Mafia* (New York: Columbia University Press, 2009), 256.

20. Giuseppe Carlo Marino, *Storia della mafia* (Rome: Newton Compton editori, 1988), 210.

21. Ibid., 224.

22. Crisiano Armati and Yari Selvetella, *Roma criminale* (Newton Compton editori, Roma, 2005), 249 ff.

23. Lupo, *Quando la mafia trovò l'America,* 258 and 259.

24. Ibid., 267.

25. See "Quand les femmes prennent le pouvoir," *L'Express*, 30–32 (August 13–19 2009).

26. Saverio Lodato, *Trent'anni di mafia* (Milan: Rizzoli, 2006), 483.

27. Vittorio Paliotti, *Storia della camorra* (Rome: Newton Compton editori, 2006), 217 ff.

The Mafia's Victims and Methods of Elimination

1. John Dickie, *Cosa Nostra: A History of the Sicilian Mafia* (New York: St. Martin's Press, 2004), 143.

2. Estes Kefauver, *Crime in America* (New York: Doubleday & Co., 1959), 47.

3. Dickie, 143.

4. Vincenzo Ceruso, *Le sagrestie di Cosa Nostra* (Rome: Newton Compton editori, 2007), 50 ff.

5. Saverio Lodato, *Ho ucciso Giovanni Falcone, la confessione di Giovanni Brusca* (Milan: Mondadori, 1999) 157. The earnings of the book were donated to charity.

6. Ibid., 149.

7. Ibid., 152.

8. Ibid., 151.

9. Salvatore Lupo, *Quando la mafia trovò l'America* (Turin: Einaudi, 2008), 247 and 248.

10. Selwyn Raab, *Le famiglie di Cosa Nostra* (Rome: Newton Compton editori, 2009), 384.

11. Lupo, 262.

12. Giuseppe Carlo Marino, *Storia della mafia* (Rome: Newton Compton editori, 1998), 390 (The grounds for the judgment of the tribunal of Palermo of October 23, 1999).

13. Rosario Poma and Enzo Perrone, *La mafia, nonni e nipoti* (Florence: Vallecchi, 1971), 42.

14. Lupo, 302.

The War on the Mafia: Judges and Policemen Alone Against the Octopus

1. Paolo Morello, *Briganti, fotografia e malavita nella Sicilia dell'Ottocento* (Palermo: Sellerio, 1999), 20 ff.

2. Morello, 86.

3. Selwyn Raab, *Le famiglie di Cosa Nostra* (Rome: Newton Compton editori, 2009), 32.

4. Pietro Lauro, *Classe dirigente, mafia e fascismo 1920-1924* (Palermo: Sellerio, 1988), 26.

5. Michele Pantaleone, *The Mafia and Politics* (New York: Coward-McCann, 1966), 32.

6. Salvatore Lupo, *History of the Mafia* (New York: Columbia University Press, 2009), 210 and 214.

7. Pantaleone, 39

8. Cesare Mori, *The Last Struggle with the Mafia* (London: Putnam, 1933), 354–55.

9. Pantaleone, 42.

10. Felice Cavallaro, *Mafia album di Cosa Nostra* (Milan: Rizzoli, 1992), 215.

11. Giuseppe Carlo Marino, *Storia della mafia* (Rome: Newton Compton editori, 1998), 224.

12. Rosario Poma and Enzo Perrone, *La mafia, nonni e nipoti* (Florence: Vallecchi, 1971), 293.

13. Alexander Stille, *Nella terra degli infedeli* (Milan: Mondadori, 1995), 152.

14. Lupo, 293.

15. Ibid., 292.

The Great *Pentiti*: from Tommaso Buscetta to Giovanni Brusca

1. Salvatore Lupo, *History of the Mafia* (New York: Columbia University Press, 2009), 296.

2. On this point see Felice Cavallaro, *Mafia album di Cosa Nostra* (Milan: Rizzoli, 1992), 140 ff, and Petra Reski, *Santa Mafia* (Modena: Edizioni Nuovi Mondi, 2009), 106.

3. Giuseppe Carlo Marino, *Storia della mafia* (Rome: Newton Compton editori, 1998), 245.

4. John Dickie, *Cosa Nostra: A History of the Sicilian Mafia* (New York: St. Martin's Press, 2004), 134 and 135.

5. Michele Pantaleone, *The Mafia and Politics* (New York: Coward-McCann, 1966), 11.

6. Saverio Lodato, *Trent'anni di mafia* (Milan: Rizzoli, 2006), 24.

7. Ibid., 25.

8. Lupo, 297.

9. From the text of the confession of July 21, 1984, and the days following, as reported by Salvatore Lupo in *Che cosa è la mafia*, 21.

10. Dickie, 36.

11. Alexander Stille, *Nella terra degli infedeli* (Milan: Mondadori, 1995), 282.

12. Saverio Lodato, *Ho ucciso Giovanni Falcone, la confessione di Giovanni Brusca* (Milan: Mondadori, 1999), 9.

13. Ibid., 86 and 87.

14. Dickie, 34.

The Financial Organization of the Mafia

1. Martin Short, *The Rise of the Mafia* (London: John Blake Publishing Ltd, 2009), 302.

2. Selwyn Raab, *Le famiglie di Cosa Nostra* (Rome: Newton Compton editori, 2009), 178.

3. Giuseppe Carlo Marino, *Storia della mafia* (Rome: Newton Compton editori, 1998), 259.

4. On this point, see, among others, D. Saubaber, "Le vrai pouvoir des mafias," *L'Express* (August 7, 2008.)

5. Umberto Lucentini, *Paolo Borsellino, il valore di una vita* (Milan: San Paolo edizioni, 2006), 291.

6. Enzo Ciconte, *N'drangheta dall'Unità a oggi* (Rome-Bari: Editori Laterza, 1992), 362.

7. Petra Reski, *Santa Mafia* (Modena: Edizioni Nuovi Mondi, 2009), 15 and 16.

8. Vittorio Paliotti, *Storia della camorra* (Rome: Newton Compton editori, 2006), 15.

9. On the activities of the Casalesi clan, see the reconstruction of Rosaria Capacchione, *L'oro della camorra* (Milan: Biblioteca Universale Rizzoli, 2008).

10. Elio Veltri and Antonio Laudati, *Mafia Pulita* (Milan: Longanesi, 2009), 114.

11. See *La Repubblica* (December 23, 2009), 29.

12. On this subject, see the report prepared by Censis (Centro Studi Investimenti Sociali) in September 2009 for the Parliamentary Commission for the Investigation of the Mafia.

13. BBC News, *Mafia: "boosted" by credit crisis*, broadcast November 12, 2008.

14. Short, 308.

15. Compare the report on the actions and results of the security-related activities of the Ministry of the Interior (August 15, 2009).

16. Veltri and Laudati, 73.

The International Mafias, from the Japanese Yakuza to the Russian and Chinese Mafias

1. Giuseppe Carlo Marino, *Storia della mafia* (Rome: Newton Compton editori, 1998), 358 ff.

2. Elio Veltri and Antonio Laudati, *Mafia Pulita* (Milan: Longanesi, 2009), 45 and 46.

3. Marino, 368.

4. Ibid., 369.

5. Veltri and Laudati, 153.

6. Ibid., 185 and 186.

7. See F. Mastrogiovanni, "Narcos e 'Ndrangheta i fratelli della droga," *Il fatto quotidiano* (December 23, 2009).

The Mafia and Film

1. See the film review by Roberto Saviano, "Letter all'Italia Infelice," *L'Espresso*, 42 (October 22, 2009).

GLOSSARY

Associates: Those who have undergone the rite of membership, a ceremony that formalizes the entry of a new member (associate) in a Mafia organization. The procedures and exact wording of the oath to be sworn vary according to the particular organization and are surrounded by secrecy.

AMGOT (Allied Military Government of Occupied Territories): The administrative structure created by the Allied armies in order to ensure a form of provisional government in certain European countries recently liberated, such as Italy.

Black Hand: A criminal gang composed mainly of immigrants who landed in New York in the late nineteenth century. They specialized in the extortion of merchants and businessmen of Italian origin in the United States.

Bootleggers: Smugglers of alcoholic beverages in the United States during the period known as Prohibition (January 1920 to December 1933). One result of the Volstead Act, which prohibited the importing of alcohol, was a system of smuggling that not only involved the secret delivery of illegal merchandise but also caused a drop in the customs fees normally collected on legal imports.

Boss: The English word most commonly used in Italian to indicate in a general way someone who occupies a position at the top of a criminal organization and also someone within the Cosa Nostra and the Sicilian Mafia specifically. The heads of the most important families were called *padrino* (godfather), while a *capo mafia* (Mafia boss) was someone who could assume command of one of the groups that made up a family. The *Capo dei Capi* (boss of bosses) was the person at the head of the Commission or Cupola (see below).

Camorra: A Mafia-type criminal organization active in Naples and the Campania region of Italy.

Campiere: A private guard employed to maintain security on a landed estate, usually under the command of a *gabellotto* (see below). The *campiere* was a minor figure in the Mafia hierarchy in the Sicilian countryside.

Capo dei Capi (boss of bosses): The top person in the Commission or Cupola, the coordinating body of the Sicilian Mafia. A *capo mafia* is the boss of a single family or of one of the clans that make up a family.

Cartels (in Spanish, *carteles*): Criminal organizations in South America specialized in drug trafficking, cocaine in particular, such as those that operated in Colombia in the 1980s and 1990s (Medellin cartel, Cali cartel). The Spanish term also refers to smaller-size clans that appeared in the region.

Chinese Triad: A Mafia-type organized crime group in China; the general name for all such groups in China.

Commission of the Cosa Nostra: A crime syndicate created in the early 1930s in order to keep the peace and coordinate the sharing of interests and territory among the families of the Italian-American Mafia.

Consigliere: Sicilian dialect indicating the person on the Commission of the Cosa Nostra responsible for mediating conflicts among the Mafia families.

Cosa Nostra: The name of the Italian-American Mafia. In 1963, the *pentito* Joe Valachi publicly revealed the existence of a secret society with that name, made up of immigrants from Sicily and operating in the United States for criminal purposes. The different Italian-American Mafia gangs had specific names according to the city in which they conducted their business, for example, "the Outfit" in Chicago and "the Arm" in Buffalo. From the 1980s, following the statements made by many *pentiti*, the term Cosa Nostra was also used for the Sicilian Mafia, illustrating how the groups in both countries continued to influence one another. This book has used Cosa Nostra to refer to the U.S. organization only to avoid confusion with the Sicilian Mafia.

Cosche: Italian word referring to the gangs that form the nucleus of the Sicilian Mafia. These groups, formed by families or by individuals united by social bonds or by personal acquaintance, comprise the clans that are part of the internal hierarchical structure of the organization. *Cosca*, in Sicilian dialect, refers to the crown of leaves on an artichoke and symbolizes the strong union that exists among those who belong to the Mafia.

Cupola: Word commonly used to refer to the Commission composed of bosses from the different provinces of Sicily that coordinated Mafia activities.

Eco-Mafia: The activities of groups and families connected primarily to the Neapolitan Camorra and the Calabrian 'Ndrangheta that made money in the illegal trafficking of municipal and industrial waste harmful to human health.

Excellent cadavers: This expression came into common use through the Italian media. It is used to indicate victims of organized crime who had occupied important government posts, such as politicians, judges, and high-ranking members of the police.

Federación: The name given to the unified command formed by the criminal cartels in South America in order to share the market for the transport and sale of drugs.

Feud: A struggle between rival groups of Mafia families fed by revenge and reprisals. The term comes from a medieval Germanic law by which a state of enmity or private war between families would be cured through personal vengeance.

French Connection: The name given to a trading network used by the Mafia and other criminal organizations in order to manage the heroin traffic between Europe and the United States up until the early 1970s. The pure product that came from the Middle and Far East was refined in France and then exported to the United States.

"Friends of friends": An expression that indicates membership in the politico-mafioso system that revolves around the business dealings of the Mafia. To be a "friend of friends" means to be part of a network of reciprocal interests and illegal complicity. The phrase was used perhaps for the first time by Vincenzo di Giovanni, a seventeenth-century scholar and historian of Sicily. In a manuscript dedicated to Palermo and to the community of bankers and merchants from Pisa who had established themselves in Sicily, he praises one of those fine gentlemen as a "great friend of friends." Amigos dos Amigos, in Portuguese, is the name of one of the Mafia-type organizations that engages in drug trafficking in the favelas of Rio de Janeiro in Brazil.

Gabellotto: Someone who rented a portion of a landed estate from one of the large Sicilian landowners against payment of a sum of money known as the *gabella*. The *gabellotto* was at the top of a feudal system, based on the exploitation of the peasants, which characterized the birth of the Mafia in the countryside.

Golden Triangle: An area in South East Asia, including parts of Burma, Laos, and Thailand, that up to the end of the 1990s produced more opium than any other part of the world.

Indirect Revenge: It is exacted by the Mafia through the murder of relatives or other persons very close to a *pentito* who has decided to cooperate with the authorities.

Mafia: The term for the criminal organization that developed in western Sicily from the second half of the nineteenth century. The same word is often used to indicate groups joined in secret associations dedicated to illegal activities in other countries, such as the Russian, Chinese, and Japanese Mafias. These other groups have initiation rites, unwritten rules, and other methods similar to those used by the Sicilian Mafia.

Men of honor: The name by which those who have sworn an oath to the Mafia and become part of the organization refer to themselves. The adjective "mafioso," like the word "Mafia" itself, is not part of the vocabulary used in the world of the gangs, in which the "Mafia," understood in the criminal sense of the term, does not exist. It is rather a "state within the state," which follows its own rules and has its own "code of honor."

MIS: Italian abbreviation for the *Movimento Indipendentista Siciliano* (Independence Movement of Sicily), a political group active in Sicily especially after the Allied landings in 1943. It called for the separation of Sicily from Italy and from the central government in Rome. It had at its disposal a group of armed volunteers under the command of the bandit Salvatore Giuliano, the perpetrator of the Massacre of Portella della Ginestra in 1947.

Money laundering: Various financial transactions by which criminal organizations seek to hide the illegal sources of their money and invest it in legal activities. Examples include the export of currency to so-called "fiscal paradises" with fewer regulations on investing, as well as the purchase of businesses such as supermarkets, restaurants, and bars.

Murder, Inc.: Nickname given by an American journalist to an independent gang of hit men that operated in New York in the 1930s in the service of various criminal groups, including the Cosa Nostra.

'Ndrangheta: A criminal organization similar to the Mafia active in the Italian region of Calabria.

Omertà: An Italian word for the Sicilian Mafia's ironclad law of silence that requires absolute secrecy about the organization and its criminal activities, on pain of death for anyone who violates it.

Operation Husky: Code name for the Anglo-American landings in Sicily in July 1943.

Organizatsya: One of the names for the Mafia-type criminal organization in Russia, also known as the *Mafiya*.

OSS (Office of Strategic Services): A U.S. secret service agency that was a precursor to the CIA (Central Intelligence Agency), active in Sicily during World War II.

Padrino: The Italian word for godfather, which by now has become part of the mythology of the Mafia, and refers to the most powerful bosses of the Sicilian Mafia families. It derives from the word *parrinu*, which in Sicilian dialect means priest. The religious connotations help to suggest the idea of a boss to whom one can confide problems, and from whom one can obtain help and justice against any kind of abuse.

Pentito: Italian for someone who repents or a turncoat. It refers to a Mafioso who decides to cooperate with the authorities, confessing his crimes and providing information useful in fighting the organization. Many *pentiti*, such as Tommaso Buscetta, did not cooperate out of remorse or due to any sense of morality, but rather in reaction to a betrayal suffered or to an order given by the organization calling for the murder of a relative. *Pentiti* would receive a greatly reduced sentence as well as entry in a witness protection program for themselves and their families, which would continue even after their release from prison.

Picciotti: Italian term meaning soldiers.

Pizza Connection: The name of an investigation into heroin trafficking between Italy and the United States that began in July 1979, conducted by police from both countries. It refers to the pizza parlors in New York that were used as a cover for distribution of the drugs.

Pizzo: Italian slang for the "tax"—i.e., protection money—imposed by the Mafia and other Italian criminal organizations such as the Neapolitan Camorra and the Calabrian 'Ndrangheta by means of blackmail and intimidation of those who engage in commercial and industrial activities, or who practice one of the liberal professions. In exchange for money, the gangs guarantee protection from the attacks, threats, and physical violence that are used to punish anyone who refuses to obey the law of the rackets.

Sacra Corona Unita: A criminal organization similar to the Mafia based in the Italian region of Puglia.

Testimone di giustizia: A witness who provides important information to the judges in their fight against the Mafia. Such a witness receives special protection but, unlike a *pentito*, has not committed any crime.

Volstead Act: A law that went into effect in 1920, following the ratification one year earlier of the Eighteenth Amendment to the United States Constitution. It prohibited the manufacture, sale, transport, import, and export of alcoholic beverages in all territories of the United States. The act marks the start of prohibition.

White Hand: An association formed by businessmen who wanted to oppose the Black Hand. They would lend money to victims of blackmail and usury.

White-gloved High Mafia: Refers to the upper level of the criminal hierarchy in Sicily, which also included politicians and corrupt public officials. The term comes from the fact that at one time gloves of this color were considered the most precious and therefore worn only by rich and very important people.

X-2: A counterespionage service of the OSS (see above).

Yakuza: Refers to an individual Japanese mafioso and to the entire criminal organization in Japan similar to the Mafia.

INDEX

The page numbers in bold refer to the images in which the person appears.

Photographic credits:
All photographs © SCALA, Florence; ANSA/SCALA, Florence; AGF/SCALA, Florence; De Agostini/SCALA, Florence; WhiteImages/SCALA, Florence; Heritage Images/SCALA, Florence; with the exception of Universal/The Kobal Collection, pp. 192–193; Warner Bros/First National/The Kobal Collection, p.194; Paramount/The Kobal Collection, pp.197 and 198; HBO/The Kobal Collection, p.199.

Translated from the Italian by Brian Eskenazi
Design: www.francism.com
Copyediting: Lindsay Porter
Typesetting: Claude-Olivier Four
Proofreading: Chrisoula Petridis
Color Separation: MCP Jouve
Printed in Spain by Dédalo

Text © SCALA GROUP Spa

Simultaneously published in French as *Mafia. Histoire et Mythologie*
© Flammarion, S.A., Paris, 2011

English-language edition
© Flammarion, S.A., Paris, 2011

11 12 13 3 2 1

ISBN: 978-2-08-030150-5
Dépôt légal: 09/2011